barefoot contessa
back to basics

barefoot contessa back to basics

Fabulous Flavor from Simple Ingredients

Ina Garten

PHOTOGRAPHS BY QUENTIN BACON

Clarkson Potter/Publishers

New York

Published in the United States by Clarkson Potter/Publishers, an
imprint of the Crown Publishing Group, a division of Random House,
Inc., New York.
www.crownpublishing.com
www.clarksonpotter.com

CLARKSON POTTER is a trademark and POTTER with colophon is a
registered trademark of Random House, Inc.

Library of Congress Cataloging-in-Publication Data
Garten, Ina.
    Barefoot Contessa back to basics: fabulous flavor from simple
ingredients / Ina Garten; photographs by Quentin Bacon.—1st ed.
    p.   cm.
    Includes index.
    1. Cookery.   2. Barefoot Contessa (Store).   I. Title.
TX714.G3635   2008
641.5—dc22   2008010658

ISBN 978-1-4000-5435-0

Printed in Japan
Food styling by Cyd McDowell
Prop styling by Philippa Brathwaite

10 9 8 7 6 5 4 3 2

First Edition

For Anna Pump

who taught me that simple food has the most style

contents

thanks!

One of the pleasures of writing cookbooks is that it's this handmade object in a world where everything's manufactured. I particularly love that I get to collaborate with so many people who I adore and admire, and the result is better than what any one of us alone could have created. First and foremost, I want to thank my dear friend Sarah Chase, who writes wonderful cookbooks (*Nantucket Open-House Cookbook* among others) and who constantly inspires me with her recipes and ideas. I also want to thank my assistant, Barbara Libath, who's by my side all day every day shopping, baking, tweaking, and suggesting until the recipe I have in mind is exactly right.

For me, photographs are a very important part of my cookbooks; I want you to see the photograph and feel like licking the page. My friend Quentin Bacon takes the most beautiful photographs. Cyd McDowell makes luscious food and Philippa Brathwaite brings beautiful china and linens for us to use. Some of my happiest days are the ones we spend working together.

And then there's the book itself; my brilliant editor, Pam Krauss, knows exactly when to say the right word to keep me on track and when to step out of harm's way when my obsessions kick in. She makes me look so much smarter than I am. Marysarah Quinn and I have more fun than should be legal working on the book design together; thank you for putting up with me. And thank you to Lauren Shakely at Clarkson Potter and Jenny Frost at Crown for always believing in me. And of course, my wonderful agent, Esther Newberg, who is always on my side, no matter what.

And finally, there's my sweet husband, Jeffrey, who, no matter what I serve him, thinks it's the most delicious thing he's ever eaten. I love making him happy and his delight keeps me looking for the best recipes I can possibly make.

introduction

People are always asking me

what the new food trends are, but I have to admit that food trends really don't interest me. One year, everyone's cooking with foam. The next year, they're doing improbable flavor combinations like oyster ice cream. Ugh—no, thank you! It turns out that what I need from a recipe is pretty simple: I want an easy recipe that I can hopefully make in advance, and when friends arrive, I want the house to smell wonderful. (And I wouldn't mind if they thought I was a great cook, too.) That's not too much to ask, is it? Maybe that's why I'm far less excited by trendy new ingredients or fussy cooking techniques than I am by the basics; I don't see any reason why we can't buy perfectly good ingredients in a grocery store, cook them simply, and serve an absolutely delicious meal that will delight everyone at the table.

I want the house to be filled with delicious smells.

When I talk about getting back to basics, though, I'm not talking about simple mashed potatoes or a plain roast chicken. What truly fires my imagination is taking ordinary ingredients and cooking them—or pairing them—in a way that "unlocks" their true flavors. What turns a loin of pork into a delicious roast that tastes rich and full of flavor? How can I transform a butternut squash into a silky soup with a balance of spicy and sweet—or a salad that pushes the squash's flavor in an entirely different direction without overpowering it? Cinnamon in an apple pie can overwhelm the delicate apple flavors, but my Apple Dried Cherry Turnovers (page 196) have a touch of cinnamon

to bring out the "appleness," combined with sugar and a buttery crust. They fill my house with the tart-sweet smell of baking apples, and nothing I add will make that taste any better.

The same goes for the cooking techniques I rely on. Other than a standing mixer and a food processor, I rarely use any appliance more high-tech than a food mill or a mandoline. I care about the quality of the ingredients I buy, and you'll find tips throughout this book that will help you get the best out of your purchases, too, as well as answers to some of the most common questions I've been asked over the years. (When you own a specialty food store, as I did for almost twenty years, you get asked every imaginable question. Also, when you need to dice fifty pounds of butternut squash, you figure out pretty quickly the fastest way to peel a butternut squash without losing a finger.) Each recipe has tips on how to know when you've done it right.

Instead of looking for new ideas, I'm just looking for old ideas and finding the best ways to make delicious food. That's what I mean by getting back to basics. I hope you enjoy making lots of the recipes in this book, that your house is filled with wonderful smells, and that your friends think you're brilliant, too.

in search of flavor

There are so many ways to unlock the flavor of food and it's the thing I'm always exploring when I cook. Close your eyes the next time you eat a piece of chocolate cake; did it *really* taste like chocolate or did the fudgey-looking icing just trick you into thinking it would taste like chocolate? The best chocolate desserts have a depth of flavor that hits you in a few ways—both sweet and bitter, with a winey complexity—and it's my goal to bring out that complexity to reveal the true essence of chocolate in my chocolate desserts. Every dish in this book has one special element that brings out its true essence.

Sometimes it's not something in the dish, but how you "finish" the dish that makes the difference. A friend once mentioned that she had made my Orzo with Roasted Vegetables from *Barefoot Contessa Parties* many times, and although it was always delicious, she felt it somehow tasted better when I made it. Her comment gave me pause because my friend's a wonderful cook and there's nothing very tricky about that recipe—it's eggplant, peppers, lemons, orzo. So why would hers taste different from mine?

A few months later, totally by chance, I was entertaining a large group of friends and I asked a caterer to cook for us. My favorite standby was on the menu again: Orzo with Roasted Vegetables. And sure enough, when I tried a bite it didn't have the bright, fresh, edgy flavor that I like; for lack of a better word, there was a kind of flatness to the dish. I was reminded of my friend's comment and it really got me thinking.

What I ultimately realized is that not only do I taste things for seasoning along the way, but I also give every dish a final taste to see if it doesn't need one more jolt of flavor, something to wake it up. When I make that Orzo with Roasted Vegetables, nine times out of ten I feel that it needs an extra splash of freshly squeezed lemon juice and a sprinkling of sea salt. Just that small last-minute addition gives the dish a fresh and—I would say—"bright" flavor. There's a lot of lemon juice in the dish already, but it's the last splash of lemon that hits your tongue first. You'll be surprised how small adjustments like these made right before serving really boost the flavor of your cooking.

My new barn is a big kitchen where
everyone can cook together. For barn
sources and resources, see page 263.

cooking seasonally

Each ingredient has a season and that's generally the time it's most flavorful.

Of course the search for flavor starts at the beginning: in the shopping. In the U.S. we can buy almost any ingredient any time of the year. Fresh strawberries in December? No problem! They're flown in from California. Lamb in summer? It's shipped in from New Zealand. But each ingredient has a season and that's generally the time it's most flavorful. Not only is it more likely to be grown or raised locally—and ripened on the vine—it's also likely to be fresher and less expensive. I admit that cooking this way didn't always come naturally to me. Jeffrey and I have been lucky to have a little apartment in Paris right in front of one of the best street markets in the city. I'd always dreamed of cooking like a real Frenchwoman, marketing each morning and making simple, savory meals each night, but much to my surprise, I found it incredibly stressful. It's not that people there cook seasonally; it's that cooking seasonally is the *only* option. You go to the market in October and there are a dozen kinds of wild mushrooms but no greens. In winter, French markets have potatoes and apples, and in summer, there are heirloom tomatoes and fresh peaches. You can't buy raspberries in December or pears in July—and why should you? What's in season is plentiful and full of flavor, and you don't have to do much to make it taste great. But coming from the U.S., I found this kind of spontaneous menu planning hard and I tended to fall back on my favorite tried-and-true American recipes no matter what the season.

Then, one day, I decided to make Thanksgiving dinner for friends in Paris. The French markets have wonderful free-range turkeys, so that wasn't a problem. But cranberries? I looked everywhere and the only place I could find them was in a friend's freezer. The season for Brussels sprouts was over so I had a vegetable crisis. And since pumpkin isn't even sold in France I had to make do with a French squash called potiron. Exhausted, I reluctantly came to the conclusion that I needed to start cooking like a French person, forcing myself to go to the market without any idea of what I would make and simply

cooking with the ingredients I found there. It was like jumping off a cliff and it was scary, but it was exciting, too. Ultimately it taught me how to buy what's plentiful, which turns out to be exactly what tastes best. My recipes for Roasted Potato Leek Soup (page 63) and Easy Sole Meunière (page 131) came out of that trip and they're now among our favorite dishes.

cooking for flavor

I hate muddled flavors: I don't add lemongrass to chicken to give it flavor; I want the intrinsic flavor of the chicken to come out through seasoning, marinating, roasting—whatever makes the chicken taste exactly how it wants to be. It's food with integrity, served in season, and flavored with respect for the ingredients. While you don't need to do much to make great seasonal produce taste amazing—who can improve on a perfect ear of summer corn or briny fresh sea scallops—what about the everyday ingredients that we all use day in, day out?

A process rather than an ingredient can also make all the difference. I use slow roasting to concentrate the tomato essence for Roasted Tomatoes with Basil (page 183) and high-temperature roasting for Roasted Parsnips & Carrots (page 179). Searing and marinating are good for poultry and meats, as in the Coq au Vin (page 115) and Herb-Marinated Loin of Pork (page 126). Another important step is allowing meat or fish to "rest" before carving it. This resting period allows the juices to be absorbed back into the meat, which makes it so much more flavorful than if you'd served it right off the grill or out of the oven.

But mostly it's about cooking with the ingredients that bring out the essence of any dish. Judy Rodgers at Zuni Café in San Francisco told me that the secret to her famous (and deeply delicious) roast chicken is salting the chicken when it arrives at the restaurant before it's stored in the refrigerator. That way the salt really gets into the meat and gives it great flavor when it's cooked. (You can use this technique with almost any meat, poultry, or fish.) My friend Sarah Leah Chase adds Cassis liqueur to her Plum Crunch (page 205) to bring out the plums' essential "pluminess"—and you don't even know the cassis is in there.

Many dishes that I make rely on one or two ingredients to really amp up the flavor at the end, and it's almost always an ingredient that's already in the dish. My Caesar salad has plenty of Parmesan in the dressing but it's a final sprinkle of ground Parmesan that gives the flavor, the saltiness, and also—very importantly—the texture of fresh Parmesan on the tongue. My lentil soup is rich and delicious but a splash of good red wine vinegar at the end perks up the flavor and gives the soup an edge. The first few times I made the Cream of Fresh Tomato Soup (page 59) for this book, it was a bit flat; it had lots of fresh tomato flavor but it needed a little heat at the end. I was amazed how six grinds of the pepper mill could give a whole pot of soup the depth of flavor I was looking for.

Tomato Caprese salad can be just okay or absolutely delicious, depending on how you use the ingredients.

A perfect example of this philosophy is the simplest of dishes, tomato Caprese salad—tomatoes, mozzarella, and basil. It can be just okay or it can be absolutely delicious, depending on how you use the ingredients. Recently, I was served a beautifully arranged Caprese salad—thinly sliced tomatoes and mozzarella with a beautiful chiffonade of basil on top. It should have been delicious but it was just plain boring. I realized that when I make it, I use big, thick slices of good red summer tomatoes plus chunky wedges of green zebra tomatoes and halved small yellow pear tomatoes. The contrast in flavors and textures of the tomatoes is wonderful. The tomatoes are layered with thick, creamy slices of fresh salted mozzarella and big shreds of spicy basil leaves. Finally, a drizzle of syrupy balsamic vinegar and a fruity olive oil, big flakes of crunchy sea salt, and coarse grinds of spicy black pepper contribute both flavor and texture. Using almost exactly the same ingredients as in the boring salad, and with no more effort, you can serve your guests something absolutely delicious.

the magic ingredient

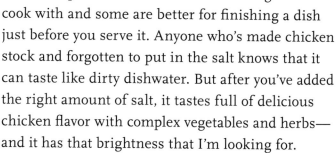

There are lots of ingredients that can unlock flavors, but if I were stuck on the proverbial desert island, I'd definitely have to bring salt with me. Not traditional "table salt" but rather kosher salt, sea salt, or a very briny French sea salt called fleur de sel. Each one has its own place in a dish. Some salts are good to

cook with and some are better for finishing a dish just before you serve it. Anyone who's made chicken stock and forgotten to put in the salt knows that it can taste like dirty dishwater. But after you've added the right amount of salt, it tastes full of delicious chicken flavor with complex vegetables and herbs—and it has that brightness that I'm looking for.

Another important ingredient is Parmesan cheese. You'd be amazed how many times I've made something and felt the flavor or the texture was just missing something. I stand in front of the refrigerator looking for inspiration, hoping to find something that will do the trick. And there it is: Reggiano Parmesan cheese from Italy. Even a little bit can be spicy and full of flavor, and if it's ground correctly, it also has a wonderful texture. I love ground Parmesan cheese in Spring Green Risotto (page 147) or big gratings of Parmesan on a Roasted Butternut Squash Salad (page 88). It gives the dishes flavor and texture that are amazing.

Other things I reach for often to add flavor include good wine vinegar or freshly squeezed lemon juice (to give a dish a sharper edge), Pernod (to bump up the anise flavor in dishes with fennel), coffee (to intensify the taste of chocolate), and a tablespoon of butter or cream (to round out the flavor). When you're cooking, stop at the end and taste the dish—*really* taste it. Does it have depth of flavor? Can you taste the lemon in the lemon capellini with your eyes closed? Does the chocolate flavor hit you just once and fade away or is it complex enough to linger on your tongue?

garnishing

The next detail in the flavor parade is how you serve the dishes you've spent so much time cooking. Twenty years ago, every platter was garnished with parsley. Parsley certainly has a pleasant, herby flavor but not for every dish! In the 1990s, edible flowers seemed to be the garnish of choice. I hate flowers on food. What do flowers say about the flavors in a dish? What I always use to garnish a dish— and only if it *needs* a garnish—is an ingredient that's actually *in* the dish. For example, the Provençal butter I put on my French Bistro Steaks (page 122) is made with fresh thyme, so I like to put a few sprigs of thyme on the plate. Your eyes tell your palate to expect the flavor of thyme, and when you smell the thyme as the plate is served you also start to "taste" the thyme in your mind even before you've begun to eat. White Pizzas with Arugula (page 82) are topped with arugula dressed with a lemon vinaigrette, so I'll sometimes throw a slice of lemon into the salad before serving. You see the pizza, the cheeses, and the arugula but now you also know to expect fresh lemon in the dressing.

making a menu

Finally, I think about how the dishes I cook will taste together. We've all planned dinner parties when we wanted to wow our friends and pulled out all the stops—the best dishes we know how to make, all together in one menu. It's too many right things together and your guests go home holding their bellies. I know. I've done it myself. It's far better to create a menu of dishes that complement one another—three or four things that want to be together. Not every dish has to be a star; I choose one special dish and design the rest of the menu around it. And remember, the star doesn't always have to be the entrée or a meat dish; it can be a vegetable or a starch that your guests will remember.

I had a dinner party for very special friends and I wanted the meal to be memorable. I decided Tagliarelle with Truffle Butter (page 152) would be the showpiece of the meal. To balance the luxuriousness of the truffles, I chose a simple Roast Capon (*Barefoot Contessa at Home*) cooked on a bed of onions without any gravy because the pasta sauce was rich enough. For the vegetable, I chose Roasted Carrots (*The Barefoot Contessa Cookbook*) cooked at a high temperature because the sweetness of the caramelized carrots would balance the creaminess of the pasta and the woodsy flavor of the truffles. I even left out the green herbs for the carrots because I didn't want them competing with the fresh chives on the pasta. And since the meal was quite rich, instead of a cake or pudding for dessert, I made the very thinnest French Apple Tart (page 191). Each dish was simple and it all worked really well together. I don't think anyone went home disappointed that night.

When I'm writing a menu, I like dishes that have an affinity for one another. Herb-Marinated Loin of Pork (page 126) just naturally goes with Celery Root & Apple Purée (page 169). A simple Roasted Turkey Roulade (page 109) wants to be with Maple-Roasted Butternut Squash (page 158). They're in season at the same time and they belong together. Crisp Macoun apples served with sharp English farmhouse Cheddar just *sound* good. They make your mouth water. You feel good when you eat them. You don't have to stop and think about how they'd taste together; you just know it will be delicious.

In the recipes that follow, I've included lots of notes about what I add to make these dishes sing and what I serve together. I hope you'll find that these little thoughts bring out the best in your cooking skills and delight your guests. Over the years they've made all the difference in the way I cook, and I hope they'll do the same for you.

I've included lots of notes about what I add to make these dishes sing.

cocktail hour

parmesan & thyme crackers

campari orange spritzer

gravlax with mustard sauce

juice of a few flowers

roasted shrimp cocktail

pomegranate cosmopolitans

savory palmiers

mango banana daiquiris

bruschetta with peppers & gorgonzola

10 no-cook things to serve with drinks

1 Salted Marcona almonds

2 Halved fresh figs wrapped in prosciutto

3 *Fromage blanc* mixed with chopped green herbs and salt and pepper and served with crackers

4 Smoked salmon served on buttered brown bread

5 Smoked salmon on store-bought blinis served with crème fraîche and iced vodka

6 Spicy salami with sliced hothouse cucumbers

7 Store-bought hummus topped with a drizzle of olive oil and toasted pine nuts and served with toasted pita triangles

8 Endive leaves stuffed with creamy Gorgonzola cheese

9 Foie gras, fig jam on toasts, and a glass of Sauternes

10 Cheese straws

parmesan & thyme crackers

makes 24 crackers

Whenever I go to London, I have to visit the Borough Market. I once bought delicious savory crackers that had the buttery texture of shortbread but were filled with cheeses and herbs. These Parmesan and thyme crackers are the perfect small bite with a glass of white wine or champagne before dinner.

You can make the roll ahead and freeze it for up to 6 months. Defrost overnight in the refrigerator and then slice and bake when you're ready to serve the crackers.

Grind the Parmesan in a food processor fitted with a steel blade.

  ¼ pound (1 stick) unsalted butter, at room temperature
  4 ounces freshly grated Parmesan cheese (about 1 cup)
  1 teaspoon minced fresh thyme leaves
  ½ teaspoon kosher salt
  ½ teaspoon freshly ground black pepper
  1¼ cups all-purpose flour

In the bowl of an electric mixer fitted with the paddle attachment, cream the butter for 1 minute. With the mixer on low speed, add the Parmesan, thyme, salt, and pepper and combine. With the mixer still on low, add the flour and combine until the mixture is in large crumbles, about 1 minute. If the dough is too dry, add 1 teaspoon water.

Dump the dough onto a floured board, press it into a ball, and roll into a 9-inch log. Wrap in plastic and refrigerate for at least 30 minutes or for up to 4 days.

Meanwhile, preheat the oven to 350 degrees. Cut the log into 3/8-inch-thick rounds with a small, sharp knife and place them on a sheet pan lined with parchment paper. Bake for 22 minutes, until very lightly browned. Rotate the pan once during baking. Cool and serve at room temperature.

campari orange spritzer

for each drink

Sometimes when I'm giving a lunch party, I like to serve a special drink, but no one really wants a cocktail at lunchtime. This lighter version of my favorite evening drink is so refreshing; it always makes me feel as though I'm sitting in the sun on a terrace in Italy; it's bitter and sweet and deliciously Italian.

   6 **ice cubes**
  ¼ cup Campari
  ½ cup freshly squeezed orange juice
1½ cups sparkling water such as San Pellegrino
     Orange slices, halved

Place the ice cubes in a highball glass. Add the Campari, orange juice, and San Pellegrino. Add a slice of fresh orange and serve ice-cold.

gravlax with mustard sauce

serves 20 to 30

When I bought Barefoot Contessa in 1978, this recipe of Diana Stratta's actually came with the store. Gravlax is a Swedish specialty of fresh salmon cured in salt and dill for several days and then sliced paper-thin. It's great for parties because you make it days in advance and it doesn't require any cooking at all. The sweet dark bread, spicy mustard sauce, and dill-marinated salmon are so delicious together.

    1 (3-pound) center-cut fresh salmon fillet
    1 large bunch of fresh dill, plus extra for garnish
    ½ cup kosher salt
    ½ cup sugar
    2 tablespoons white peppercorns, crushed
    1 tablespoon whole fennel seeds, crushed
      Thin, dark pumpernickel bread, for serving
      Mustard Sauce (recipe follows), for serving

I use the dense, dark pumpernickel breads that are about 4 inches square.

Using a mortar and pestle is the best way to crush whole white peppercorns and fennel seeds. You can crush them both together. A small coffee grinder, reserved exclusively for grinding spices, will also do a good job.

Cut the salmon fillet in 2 pieces crosswise and place one piece in a deep dish, skin side down. Wash and shake dry the dill and arrange it over the fish. Combine the salt, sugar, peppercorns, and fennel seeds in a small bowl and sprinkle it evenly over the dill. Place the other piece of salmon over the dill and spices, skin side up. Cover the dish with plastic wrap or aluminum foil. Place a smaller dish on top of the plastic wrap and weight it with heavy cans. Refrigerate the salmon for at least 2 to 3 days, turning it every 12 hours and basting it with the liquid that collects.

To serve, lay the salmon fillets flat on a cutting board and scrape off most of the dill and spices. Slice with a long, thin knife, as you would for smoked salmon. Lay the slices of bread on a cutting board, spread with the mustard sauce, and place a slice of salmon on top, covering the bread completely. Cut each bread slice in half, decorate with a sprig of dill, and serve at room temperature.

mustard sauce makes 1 1/2 cups

  1/2 cup Dijon mustard

  2 teaspoons dry ground mustard

  6 tablespoons sugar

  1/4 cup white wine vinegar

  2/3 cup good olive oil

  6 tablespoons chopped fresh dill

You can make this sauce a few days in advance and store it in the refrigerator.

Combine the Dijon mustard, ground mustard, sugar, and vinegar in a small bowl. Slowly whisk in the oil and stir in the chopped dill. Serve with the gravlax.

juice of a few flowers

makes 4 drinks

In the 1920s Sara and Gerald Murphy gave the most glamorous parties in the world at their beach house in East Hampton. Gerald was famous for his cocktails, although he insisted that each guest have no more than two drinks before dinner. He used to make this delicious cocktail with gin, but I've updated it with vodka. Their granddaughter, my friend Laura Donnelly, says he used to make them for the children without alcohol and serve them in big martini glasses. How charming is that?

If you want your drinks extra cold, you can freeze the martini glasses before serving.

If your juicer does not strain the juice, pass the juice through a sieve; otherwise it will clog the holes of your cocktail shaker.

- $^1/_2$ **cup freshly squeezed orange juice (2 oranges)**
- $^1/_2$ **cup freshly squeezed pink grapefruit juice (1 grapefruit)**
- $^1/_4$ **cup freshly squeezed lemon juice (1 lemon)**
- $^1/_4$ **cup freshly squeezed lime juice (2 limes)**
- 1 **cup good vodka, such as Grey Goose or Finlandia**
- **Extra lemon juice**
- **Granulated sugar**
- **Fresh mint sprigs**

Combine the orange juice, grapefruit juice, lemon juice, lime juice, and vodka in a pitcher. Dip the rims of 4 martini glasses first in a dish with lemon juice and then in a dish with sugar. Set aside to dry.

When ready to serve, place ice cubes in a cocktail shaker, add the cocktail mixture to fill the shaker three-quarters full, and shake for about 30 seconds. It's important to shake for a full 30 seconds to get the drink very cold and dilute it slightly with the ice. Pour into the sugared martini glasses and garnish with a sprig of mint. Continue filling the shaker with ice and cocktail mixture until all the drinks are poured. Serve ice-cold.

roasted shrimp cocktail

serves 6 to 8

How can you possibly improve on shrimp cocktail? Since roasted chicken breast tastes so much better than poached chicken breast, I wondered if that wouldn't be true for roasted shrimp as well—and it was. The good news is you don't have to deal with those big pots of boiling water. A nice spicy cocktail sauce for dipping makes it even more delicious.

Shrimp are randomly called "large, "extra-large," and "jumbo." To be accurate, order shrimp by the count per pound.

FOR THE SHRIMP

2 pounds (12 to 15 count) shrimp

1 tablespoon good olive oil

1/2 teaspoon kosher salt

1/2 teaspoon freshly ground black pepper

FOR THE SAUCE

1/2 cup Heinz chili sauce

1/2 cup Heinz ketchup

3 tablespoons prepared horseradish

2 teaspoons freshly squeezed lemon juice

1/2 teaspoon Worcestershire sauce

1/4 teaspoon Tabasco sauce

Preheat the oven to 400 degrees.

Peel and devein the shrimp, leaving the tails on. Place them on a sheet pan with the olive oil, salt, and pepper and spread them in one layer. Roast for 8 to 10 minutes, just until pink and firm and cooked through. Set aside to cool.

For the sauce, combine the chili sauce, ketchup, horseradish, lemon juice, Worcestershire sauce, and Tabasco. Serve as a dip with the shrimp.

pomegranate cosmopolitans

makes 6 drinks

When I'm overwhelmed (which is often!) I wonder if I need to change my life. Instead, I realize that I just need a good dinner with a dear friend and a delicious Cosmopolitan. Freshly squeezed lime juice is essential for this drink, and I also love the tartness of the pomegranate juice. And pomegranates are good for you, which cancels out the vodka, right?

2 cups good vodka, such as Grey Goose or Finlandia

1 cup Cointreau liqueur

1 cup cranberry juice cocktail, such as Ocean Spray

1/2 cup Pom Wonderful bottled pomegranate juice

1/2 cup freshly squeezed lime juice (4 limes)

Thinly sliced limes, for garnish

Combine the vodka, Cointreau, cranberry juice, pomegranate juice, and lime juice in a large pitcher. Fill a cocktail shaker half full with ice, pour the cocktail mixture in, and shake for a full 30 seconds. Pour into martini glasses, garnish with a slice of lime, and serve immediately.

Pomegranate juice is tart and sweet and so much easier to use than dealing with all those seeds.

You can make the mixture in advance and refrigerate it for a day or two. Don't freeze it or the ice won't dilute the drinks to the right consistency.

savory palmiers

makes 60 hors d'oeuvres

I love frozen puff pastry; it's easy to use and available in almost every grocery store in America. Palmiers—or elephant ears—are usually a sweet treat, but baked with pesto, goat cheese, and sun-dried tomatoes, they're perfect to serve with cocktails.

> 1 package frozen Pepperidge Farm puff pastry, defrosted
> 1/4 cup prepared pesto, store-bought or homemade (recipe follows)
> 1/2 cup crumbled goat cheese, such as Montrachet
> 1/4 cup finely chopped sun-dried tomatoes in oil, drained
> 1/4 cup toasted pine nuts (see note)
> Kosher salt

To toast pine nuts, place them in a dry sauté pan and cook over low heat, tossing often, for about 5 minutes, until golden brown.

Defrost puff pastry overnight in the refrigerator and use it very cold.

Lightly flour a board and carefully unfold one sheet of puff pastry. Roll the pastry lightly with a rolling pin until it's 9 1/2 × 11 1/2 inches. Spread the sheet of puff pastry with half the pesto, then sprinkle with half the goat cheese, half the sun-dried tomatoes, and half the pine nuts. Sprinkle with 1/4 teaspoon salt.

Working from the short ends, fold each end halfway to the center. Then fold each side again toward the center until the folded edges almost touch. Fold one side over the other and press lightly. Place on a sheet pan lined with parchment paper. Repeat for the second sheet of puff pastry using the remaining ingredients. Cover both rolls with plastic wrap and chill for at least 45 minutes.

Meanwhile, preheat the oven to 400 degrees.

Cut the prepared rolls of puff pastry into 1/4-inch-thick slices and place them faceup 2 inches apart on sheet pans lined with parchment paper. Bake for 14 minutes, until golden brown. Serve warm.

homemade pesto makes 4 cups

To clean basil, remove the leaves, swirl them in a bowl of water, then spin them very dry in a salad spinner. Store them in a closed plastic bag with a slightly damp paper towel. As long as the leaves are dry they will stay green for several days.

¼ cup walnuts

¼ cup pine nuts

3 tablespoons chopped garlic (9 cloves)

5 cups fresh basil leaves, packed

1 teaspoon kosher salt

1 teaspoon freshly ground black pepper

1½ cups good olive oil

1 cup freshly grated Parmesan cheese

Place the walnuts, pine nuts, and garlic in the bowl of a food processor fitted with a steel blade. Process for 30 seconds. Add the basil leaves, salt, and pepper. With the processor running, slowly pour the olive oil into the bowl through the feed tube and process until the pesto is finely puréed. Add the Parmesan and purée for a minute. Serve, or store the pesto in the refrigerator or freezer with a thin film of olive oil on top.

mango banana daiquiris

makes 4 drinks

I hate cocktails that have to be made one at a time. I make large batches of mango daiquiris in a blender. The rich mango flavor here is balanced by the sweetness of the banana, the tartness of the lime juice, and lots of dark rum to give it an edge. Ripe mangos are essential for that Caribbean flavor; be sure you buy them in advance and allow them to ripen.

- 2 cups chopped ripe mango (1 to 2 mangos, peeled and seeded)
- 1 ripe banana, chopped
- 1/2 cup freshly squeezed lime juice (4 limes)
- 1/4 cup sugar syrup (see note)
- 1 1/4 cups dark rum, such as Mount Gay
- Mango slices, for serving

Place the mango, banana, lime juice, sugar syrup, and rum in a blender and process until smooth. Add 2 cups of ice and process again until smooth and thick. Serve ice-cold in highball glasses with the mango slices.

To make sugar syrup, heat 1 cup sugar and 1 cup water in a small saucepan until the sugar dissolves. Chill.

Mangos are ripe when they smell like mangos and they give to the touch.

Limes give more juice when they're at room temperature.

bruschetta with peppers & gorgonzola

makes 32 to 36 appetizers

Bruschettas are a great way to use up all kinds of leftover vegetables, meats, and cheeses and make delicious hors d'oeuvres at the same time. These savory bites feature some of my favorite flavors from the Mediterranean: fruity olive oil, peppers, capers, and basil—not to mention a little melted Gorgonzola.

$^1\!/_4$ cup olive oil, plus extra for brushing bread
2 red bell peppers, seeded and cut into thin strips
2 yellow bell peppers, seeded and cut into thin strips
1 teaspoon sugar
2 tablespoons drained capers
$^1\!/_4$ cup julienned fresh basil leaves
Kosher salt and freshly ground black pepper
32 to 36 ($^1\!/_4$- to $^1\!/_2$-inch-thick) baguette slices
4 to 5 ounces creamy Gorgonzola, at room temperature

To julienne basil, stack the leaves, roll them like a cigar, and slice them across.

Preheat the oven to 375 degrees.

Heat the olive oil over medium-high heat in a large (12-inch) skillet. Add all the peppers and sauté for 12 to 15 minutes, stirring occasionally until tender. Sprinkle with the sugar and sauté for 2 to 3 more minutes. Stir in the capers and basil. Sprinkle with salt and pepper and set aside.

Arrange the bread slices in rows on sheet pans lined with parchment paper. Brush each slice lightly with olive oil and toast for 7 to 10 minutes, until lightly browned.

Top each toast with a spoonful of the pepper mixture. Dot each one with Gorgonzola. Return to the oven for a minute or two to warm the Gorgonzola. Sprinkle with salt and serve warm.

soup

lobster corn chowder

cream of fresh tomato soup

homemade chicken stock

roasted potato leek soup

chilled cucumber soup

pappa al pomodoro

roasted butternut squash soup

italian wedding soup

arrange flowers like a pro

1 When you arrive home with your flowers, cut the stems at an angle and put them immediately into water.

2 Fill the vase three-quarters full with water; flowers can be very thirsty. For tulips use a small amount of water.

3 Use warm water for everything except hydrangeas, which need hot tap water.

4 Put a splash of bleach in the vase. It will reduce bacteria, which can prevent the stems from drinking water.

5 For woody-stemmed flowers such as hydrangeas or lilacs, split the stems several inches up from the bottom. You want to expose the white inner part of the stem to water.

6 For flowers from bulbs and tubers, such as tulips and iris, score the bottoms of the stems as you might with scallions; the ends will curl up and they'll drink more water.

7 Choose a vase that allows the flowers to "breathe" rather than packing them tightly. Flowers look best arranged as they might grow in a garden. For example, tulips look more natural if they're given room to bend a little.

8 Build your arrangement in your hand, holding the stems and looking at the top of the flowers. When you're happy with the arrangement, cut all the stems to the same length. Tying the stems with raffia before putting the arrangement in a vase keeps them all in place.

9 Don't leave flowers in a warm sunny window. It will stress them.

10 For all flowers except tulips, recut the stems, clean the vase, and change the water every 2 or 3 days. Tulips can be temperamental; once they have opened, don't change the water.

lobster corn chowder

serves 6

This soup is chunky and hearty enough to serve alone for lunch with a good crusty bread. The depth of flavor comes from using the lobster shells and corncobs to make the stock that goes into the soup. An extra quarter cup of sherry added just before you serve it gives this rich soup a nice edge, which is important for the flavor. It's also a wonderful first course for dinner on a cool summer night.

3 ($1\frac{1}{2}$-pound) cooked lobsters, cracked and split

3 ears corn

FOR THE STOCK

6 tablespoons ($\frac{3}{4}$ stick) unsalted butter

1 cup chopped yellow onion

$\frac{1}{4}$ cup cream sherry

1 teaspoon sweet paprika

4 cups whole milk

2 cups heavy cream

1 cup dry white wine

FOR THE SOUP

1 tablespoon good olive oil

$\frac{1}{4}$ pound bacon, large-diced

2 cups large-diced unpeeled Yukon Gold potatoes
  (2 medium)

$1\frac{1}{2}$ cups chopped yellow onions (2 onions)

2 cups diced celery (3 to 4 stalks)

1 tablespoon kosher salt

1 teaspoon freshly ground black pepper

2 teaspoons chopped fresh chives

$\frac{1}{4}$ cup cream sherry

Remove the meat from the shells of the lobsters. Cut the meat into large cubes and place them in a bowl. Cover with plastic wrap and refrigerate. Reserve the shells and all the juices that collect.

(recipe continues)

Cut the corn kernels from the cobs and set aside, reserving the cobs separately.

For the stock, melt the butter in a stockpot or Dutch oven large enough to hold all the lobster shells and corncobs. Add the onion and cook over medium-low heat for 7 minutes, until translucent but not browned, stirring occasionally. Add the sherry and paprika and cook for 1 minute. Add the milk, cream, wine, lobster shells and their juices, and corncobs and bring to a simmer. Partially cover the pot and simmer the stock over the lowest heat for 30 minutes. (I move the pot halfway off the heat.)

Meanwhile, in another stockpot or Dutch oven, heat the oil and cook the bacon for 4 to 5 minutes over medium-low heat, until browned and crisp. Remove with a slotted spoon and reserve. Add the potatoes, onions, celery, corn kernels, salt, and pepper to the same pot and sauté for 5 minutes. When the stock is ready, remove the largest pieces of lobster shell and the corncobs with tongs and discard. Place a strainer over the soup pot and carefully pour the stock into the pot with the potatoes and corn. Simmer over low heat for 15 minutes, until the potatoes are tender. Add the cooked lobster, the chives, and the sherry and season to taste. Heat gently and serve hot with a garnish of crisp bacon.

cream of fresh tomato soup

serves 5 or 6

This is a great soup to make in September when there are still tons of vine-ripened tomatoes in the market and you've eaten your fill of tomato salads. I garnish the soup with spicy basil leaves and crunchy slices of French bread toasted with Parmesan cheese.

        3 tablespoons good olive oil
    1½ cups chopped red onions (2 onions)
        2 carrots, unpeeled and chopped
        1 tablespoon minced garlic (3 cloves)
        4 pounds vine-ripened tomatoes, coarsely chopped (5 large)
    1½ teaspoons sugar
        1 tablespoon tomato paste
    ¼ cup packed chopped fresh basil leaves
        3 cups chicken stock, preferably homemade
          (page 61)
        1 tablespoon kosher salt
        2 teaspoons freshly ground black pepper
    ¾ cup heavy cream
        Julienned fresh basil leaves, for garnish
        Parmesan Toasts (recipe follows) or croutons

There are several ways to purée a soup—in the food processor, in a blender—but for this soup, I prefer to use a food mill which strains out the skins and seeds but keeps all that full, rich tomato flavor.

I finish each serving with a sprinkling of sea salt.

Heat the olive oil in a large, heavy-bottomed pot over medium-low heat. Add the onions and carrots and sauté for about 10 minutes, until very tender. Add the garlic and cook for 1 minute. Add the tomatoes, sugar, tomato paste, basil, chicken stock, salt, and pepper and stir well. Bring the soup to a boil, lower the heat, and simmer, uncovered, for 30 to 40 minutes, until the tomatoes are very tender.

  Add the cream to the soup and process it through a food mill into a bowl, discarding only the dry pulp that's left. Reheat the soup over low heat just until hot and serve with julienned basil leaves and/or Parmesan toasts.

parmesan toasts

makes at least 20 toasts

This is a great way to use up leftover or frozen French bread. The toasts can be made a few hours in advance and can be recrisped for a few minutes in a warm oven.

1 **French baguette**
Good olive oil
Kosher salt and freshly ground black pepper
Freshly grated Parmesan cheese (see note)

Preheat the oven to 400 degrees.

Slice the baguette diagonally into ¼-inch-thick slices. Make as many slices as you like to serve with the soup.

Place the slices on a sheet pan lined with parchment paper. Brush with olive oil and sprinkle with salt and pepper. Sprinkle a thick layer of grated Parmesan on the toasts and bake for 5 to 10 minutes, until the toasts are lightly browned. Cool to room temperature.

For this recipe, the Parmesan is best grated on a box grater.

homemade chicken stock

makes 6 quarts

Nothing gives soup more flavor than homemade chicken stock. It's easy to make on a day when you're around the house; you throw the ingredients in a big stockpot and just let them simmer away for four hours. A good chicken stock is rich with chicken, vegetable, and herb flavors and will flavor anything you make with it. I always keep quarts of it in the freezer.

  3 **(5-pound) roasting chickens**
  3 **large yellow onions, unpeeled and quartered**
  6 **carrots, unpeeled and halved**
  4 **celery stalks with leaves, cut in thirds**
  4 **parsnips, unpeeled and cut in half (optional)**
20 **fresh parsley sprigs**
15 **fresh thyme sprigs**
20 **fresh dill sprigs**
  1 **head garlic, unpeeled and cut in half crosswise**
  2 **tablespoons kosher salt**
  2 **teaspoons whole black peppercorns**

Containers of chicken stock will last for 5 days refrigerated and for 6 months in the freezer.

Place the chickens, onions, carrots, celery, parsnips, parsley, thyme, dill, garlic, salt, and pepper in a 16- to 20-quart stockpot. Add 7 quarts of water and bring to a boil over high heat. Skim any foam that comes to the surface. Lower the heat and simmer, uncovered, for 4 hours.

Strain the entire contents of the pot through a colander, discarding the solids. Pack in quart containers and refrigerate. When the stock is cold, remove the surface fat and refrigerate again.

roasted potato leek soup

serves 6 to 8

In winter when it's chilly, I love to serve a good hearty soup. I'm always looking back to traditional things with an eye to giving them much more flavor. Potato leek soup was an American staple (in summer, it's served cold and called vichyssoise), but I was sure I could turn up the volume. Roasting the potatoes and leeks together, plus adding white wine, crème fraîche, and good Parmesan cheese, really did the trick. A drizzle of olive oil and a sprinkling of more Parmesan on each bowl didn't hurt, either.

- 2 pounds Yukon Gold potatoes, peeled and cut into ¾-inch chunks
- 4 cups chopped leeks, white and light green parts, cleaned of all sand (4 leeks)
- ¼ cup good olive oil
  Kosher salt and freshly ground black pepper
- 3 cups baby arugula, lightly packed
- ½ cup dry white wine, plus extra for serving
- 6 to 7 cups chicken stock, preferably homemade (page 61)
- ¾ cup heavy cream
- 8 ounces crème fraîche
- ¼ cup freshly grated Parmesan cheese, plus extra for garnish (see note)
  Crispy Shallots, optional (recipe follows)

For this soup, I grind the Parmesan cheese in a food processor fitted with the steel blade; but for the garnish, I prefer to grate it on the large holes of a box grater. Otherwise, the garnish just melts into the soup before you can serve it.

Preheat the oven to 400 degrees.

Combine the potatoes and leeks on a sheet pan in a single layer. Add the olive oil, 1 teaspoon salt, and ½ teaspoon pepper and toss to coat the vegetables evenly. Roast for 40 to 45 minutes, turning them with a spatula a few times during cooking, until very tender. Add the arugula and toss to combine. Roast for 4 to 5 more minutes, until the arugula is wilted. Remove the pan from the oven and place over two burners. Stir in the wine and 1 cup of the chicken stock and cook over low heat, scraping up any crispy roasted bits sticking to the pan.

(recipe continues)

In batches, transfer the roasted vegetables to a food processor fitted with the steel blade, adding the pan liquid and about 5 cups of the chicken stock to make a purée. Pour the purée into a large pot or Dutch oven. Continue to puree the vegetables in batches until they're all done and combined in the large pot. Add enough of the remaining 1 to 2 cups of stock to make a thick soup. Add the cream, crème fraîche, 2 teaspoons salt, and 1 teaspoon pepper and check the seasonings.

When ready to serve, reheat the soup gently and whisk in 2 tablespoons white wine and the Parmesan cheese. Serve hot with an extra grating of Parmesan cheese and crispy shallots, if using.

crispy shallots   makes about ½ cup

> 1½ cups olive oil or vegetable oil
> 3 tablespoons unsalted butter
> 5 to 6 shallots, peeled and sliced into thin rings

Heat the oil and butter in a saucepan over medium-low heat until it reaches 220 degrees on a candy thermometer.

Reduce the heat to low, add the shallots, and cook for 30 to 40 minutes, until they are a rich golden brown. The temperature should stay below 260 degrees. Stir the shallots occasionally to make sure they brown evenly. Remove them from the oil with a slotted spoon, drain well, and spread out to cool on paper towels. Once they have dried and crisped, they can be stored at room temperature, covered, for several days.

chilled cucumber soup with shrimp

serves 6

In summer, I love cold cucumber soup, but when I order it in a restaurant, it's often really boring. Adding Greek yogurt, red onion, and dill gave this soup more flavor but I found that it was still missing something. Freshly squeezed lemon juice added before serving gives it just the tartness needed to balance the sweet cucumbers.

A whole shrimp is too hard to eat in soup. I halve them horizontally.

I like the Fage Total brand of Greek yogurt.

3 (7-ounce) containers Greek yogurt
1 cup half-and-half
2 hothouse cucumbers, unpeeled, seeded and chopped
½ cup chopped red onion
6 scallions, white and green parts, chopped
4 teaspoons kosher salt
1½ teaspoons freshly ground black pepper
3 tablespoons chopped fresh dill
½ cup freshly squeezed lemon juice (4 lemons)
½ pound cooked large shrimp, halved (see note)
Thin slices of lemon, halved, for garnish
Fresh dill, for garnish

In a large mixing bowl, stir together the yogurt, half-and-half, cucumbers, red onion, scallions, salt, and pepper. Transfer the mixture in batches to the bowl of a food processor fitted with the steel blade. Process until the cucumbers are coarsely puréed and then pour into another bowl. Continue processing the soup until all of it is puréed. Fold in the dill, cover with plastic wrap, and refrigerate for at least 2 hours, until very cold.

Just before serving, stir in the lemon juice. Serve chilled, garnished with the shrimp, lemon, and fresh dill.

pappa al pomodoro

serves 6

Pappa al pomodoro *is a classic Italian tomato soup that's thickened with leftover bread. The first time I made this soup, I puréed it in a food processor fitted with a steel blade, which gave it a smooth texture. The second time I made it, I put it through a food mill, which left a little more texture. The last time I made it, though, I just beat it with a whisk right in the pot and it was coarse and chunky—perfect! The vegetables, wine, and basil give this soup lots of flavor without the addition of butter or cream.*

Instead of crushed canned tomatoes, I use whole San Marzano tomatoes.

$\frac{1}{2}$ cup good olive oil

2 cups chopped yellow onions (2 onions)

1 cup medium-diced carrots, unpeeled (3 carrots)

1 fennel bulb, trimmed, cored, and medium-diced (1$\frac{1}{2}$ cups)

4 teaspoons minced garlic (4 cloves)

3 cups (1-inch) diced ciabatta bread, crusts removed

2 (28-ounce) cans good Italian plum tomatoes (see note)

4 cups chicken stock, preferably homemade (page 61)

$\frac{1}{2}$ cup dry red wine

1 cup chopped fresh basil leaves

Kosher salt and freshly ground black pepper

$\frac{1}{2}$ cup freshly grated Parmesan cheese

FOR THE TOPPING

3 cups (1-inch) diced ciabatta bread

2 ounces thickly sliced pancetta, chopped

24 to 30 whole fresh basil leaves

3 tablespoons good olive oil, plus more for serving

Heat the oil in a large stockpot over medium heat. Add the onions, carrots, fennel, and garlic and cook over medium-low heat for 10 minutes, until tender. Add the ciabatta cubes and cook for 5 more minutes. Place the tomatoes in the bowl of a food processor fitted with the steel blade and process just until coarsely chopped. Add the tomatoes to the pot along with the chicken stock, red wine, basil, 1 tablespoon salt, and 1$\frac{1}{2}$ teaspoons pepper.

Bring the soup to a boil, lower the heat, and allow to simmer, partially covered, for 45 minutes.

Meanwhile, preheat the oven to 375 degrees.

For the topping, place the ciabatta, pancetta, and basil on a sheet pan large enough to hold them in a single layer. Drizzle with olive oil, sprinkle with salt and pepper, and toss well. Cook, stirring occasionally, for 20 to 25 minutes, until all the ingredients are crisp. The basil leaves will turn dark and crisp, which is perfectly fine. Reheat the soup, if necessary, and beat with a wire whisk until the bread is broken up. Stir in the Parmesan and taste for seasoning. Serve hot, sprinkled with the topping and drizzled with additional olive oil.

roasted butternut squash soup & curry condiments

serves 4 to 6

I adore butternut squash in any form. I've made the Butternut Squash and Apple Soup in Barefoot Contessa Parties! *so many times that I wanted to give it a new lease on life. Roasting the squash before making the soup really brings out its sweetness. And since there is spicy curry in the soup, I thought some classic bananas, coconut, and salty cashews on top would continue the Indian theme. It's so good.*

Toast coconut in a single layer on a sheet pan at 350 degrees for 5 to 10 minutes.

3 to 4 pounds butternut squash, peeled and seeded
2 yellow onions
2 McIntosh apples, peeled and cored
3 tablespoons good olive oil
  Kosher salt and freshly ground black pepper
2 to 4 cups chicken stock, preferably homemade
  (page 61)
½ teaspoon good curry powder

CONDIMENTS FOR SERVING

Scallions, white and green parts, trimmed and sliced diagonally
Flaked sweetened coconut, lightly toasted (see note)
Roasted salted cashews, toasted and chopped
Diced banana

Preheat the oven to 425 degrees.

Cut the butternut squash, onions, and apples into 1-inch cubes. Place them on a sheet pan and toss them with the olive oil, 1 teaspoon salt, and ½ teaspoon pepper. Divide the squash mixture between 2 sheet pans and spread in a single layer. Roast for 35 to 45 minutes, tossing occasionally, until very tender.

Meanwhile, heat the chicken stock to a simmer. When the vegetables are done, put them through a food mill fitted with the medium blade. (Alternatively, you can place the roasted vegetables in batches in a food processor fitted with the steel blade. Add some of the chicken stock and coarsely purée.) When all of the vegetables are processed, place them in a large pot and add enough chicken stock to make a thick soup. Add the curry powder, 1 teaspoon salt, and ½ teaspoon pepper. Taste for seasonings to be sure there's enough salt and pepper to bring out the curry flavor. Reheat and serve hot with condiments either on the side or on top of each serving.

italian wedding soup

serves 6 to 8

To get the best cheese flavor, buy Parmesan that has been aged for at least 2 years and grind it yourself in a food processor fitted with the steel blade.

Who likes standing at the stove rolling meatballs around in hot oil? Not to mention that I can never get them evenly browned. I discovered that chicken meatballs mixed with good Italian sausage have great flavor and they're so much easier to make because you bake them in the oven. This rich chicken soup is filled with lots of good things: spinach, pasta, and plenty of those spicy meatballs.

FOR THE MEATBALLS
- ³/₄ pound ground chicken
- ¹/₂ pound chicken sausage, casings removed
- ²/₃ cup fresh white bread crumbs
- 2 teaspoons minced garlic (2 cloves)
- 3 tablespoons chopped fresh parsley
- ¹/₄ cup freshly grated Pecorino Romano cheese
- ¹/₄ cup freshly grated Parmesan cheese, plus extra for serving
- 3 tablespoons milk
- 1 extra-large egg, lightly beaten
  Kosher salt and freshly ground black pepper

FOR THE SOUP
- 2 tablespoons good olive oil
- 1 cup minced yellow onion
- 1 cup ¹/₄-inch-diced carrots (3 carrots)
- ³/₄ cup ¹/₄-inch-diced celery (2 stalks)
- 10 cups Homemade Chicken Stock (page 61)
- ¹/₂ cup dry white wine
- 1 cup small pasta such as tubetini or stars
- ¹/₄ cup minced fresh dill
- 12 ounces baby spinach, washed and trimmed

Preheat the oven to 350 degrees.

For the meatballs, place the ground chicken, sausage, bread crumbs, garlic, parsley, Pecorino, Parmesan, milk, egg, 1 teaspoon salt, and $1/2$ teaspoon pepper in a bowl and combine gently with a fork. With a teaspoon, drop 1- to $1^1/4$-inch meatballs onto a sheet pan lined with parchment paper. (You should have about 40 meatballs. They don't have to be perfectly round.) Bake for 30 minutes, until cooked through and lightly browned. Set aside.

In the meantime, for the soup, heat the olive oil over medium-low heat in a large, heavy-bottomed soup pot. Add the onion, carrots, and celery and sauté until softened, 5 to 6 minutes, stirring occasionally. Add the chicken stock and wine and bring to a boil. Add the pasta to the simmering broth and cook for 6 to 8 minutes, until the pasta is tender. Add the fresh dill and then the meatballs to the soup and simmer for 1 minute. Taste for salt and pepper. Stir in the fresh spinach and cook for 1 minute, until the spinach is just wilted. Ladle into soup bowls and sprinkle each serving with extra grated Parmesan cheese.

The pasta will thicken the soup as it sits; just thin it with some water or chicken stock.

lunch

cape cod chopped salad

old-fashioned carrot salad

white pizzas with arugula

creamy cucumber salad

warm goat cheese in phyllo

roasted butternut squash salad

roasted tomato caprese salad

tomato & goat cheese tarts

truffled filet of beef sandwiches

roasted pears with blue cheese

mâche with warm brie

cook like a pro

1 Use good-quality cookware such as All-Clad, Le Creuset, and Cuisinart. Not only do they cook foods more evenly, they're also much easier to clean up!

2 Keep your knives sharp. I use Wüsthof knives and a Chef's Choice electric knife sharpener.

3 Use your knife like a saw. Instead of pressing down on it, slide it back and forth.

4 Don't buy a lot of fancy gadgets; the less kitchen equipment I have, the easier it is to find exactly what I need in the drawer.

5 Salt meats when they come home from the store and then rewrap and refrigerate them until you're ready to cook.

6 Use an oven thermometer to be sure the temperature on the oven dial is really accurate.

7 Have a stack of (13 × 18 × 1-inch) sheet pans for baking and roasting. Professionals call them half-sheet pans.

8 When meats and fish come out of the oven or off the grill, cover them tightly with aluminum foil and allow them to rest at room temperature for 15 minutes. They'll be juicier and more tender.

9 Don't follow outdated guidelines for cooking meats or they will be overcooked. Take beef out of the oven at 125 degrees for medium-rare, pork at 138 degrees, chicken at 140 degrees, and turkey at 150 degrees. They'll keep cooking while they "rest."

10 Use an instant thermometer to test whether meats are cooked by inserting it into the end (not the top) of a piece of meat; it's a more accurate way to test the interior temperature.

cape cod chopped salad

serves 4 or 5

Make this autumn salad just when you feel like eating apples and Roquefort cheese. I added toasted walnuts for the crunch, and orange juice and maple syrup in the dressing add a touch of sweetness. My assistant, Barbara, and I love a big plate of this salad for lunch.

8 ounces thick-cut bacon, such as Niman Ranch

8 ounces baby arugula

1 large Granny Smith apple, peeled and diced

$^1/_2$ cup toasted walnut halves, coarsely chopped (see note)

$^1/_2$ cup dried cranberries

6 ounces blue cheese, such as Roquefort, crumbled

FOR THE DRESSING

3 tablespoons good apple cider vinegar

1 teaspoon grated orange zest

2 tablespoons freshly squeezed orange juice

$2^1/_2$ teaspoons Dijon mustard

2 tablespoons pure maple syrup

Kosher salt

$^1/_2$ teaspoon freshly ground black pepper

$^2/_3$ cup good olive oil

Toast walnuts in a dry sauté pan over medium-low heat for 4 to 5 minutes, tossing frequently, until lightly browned.

Preheat the oven to 400 degrees.

Place a baking rack on a sheet pan and lay the bacon slices on the rack. Roast the bacon for about 20 minutes, until nicely browned. Allow to cool.

In a large bowl, toss together the arugula, apple, walnuts, cranberries, and blue cheese.

For the dressing, whisk together the vinegar, orange zest, orange juice, mustard, maple syrup, $1^1/_2$ teaspoons salt, and the pepper in a bowl. Slowly whisk in the olive oil.

Chop the bacon in large pieces and add it to the salad. Toss the salad with just enough dressing to moisten. Sprinkle with $^1/_2$ teaspoon salt and toss well. Serve immediately.

old-fashioned carrot salad

serves 6

Here is the perfect example of a simple recipe that, depending on the quality of the ingredients you choose, can be really boring or absolutely scrumptious. First, the carrots should be topped carrots (the ones that come with their green tops) because they really are sweeter than the bagged ones. Good mayonnaise goes without saying—I like Hellmann's or Duke's. There is no substitute for the flavor and acidity of freshly squeezed lemon juice. And finally, a golden pineapple is so much sweeter and juicier than a traditional Hawaiian pineapple.

If you place the
carrots on their side
in the feed tube and
use the coarsest
grater disk, you'll get
nice long shreds.

> $^{1}/_{2}$ cup golden raisins
> 2 pounds carrots, unpeeled
> 3 tablespoons sugar
> 3 tablespoons freshly squeezed lemon juice
> $^{1}/_{4}$ cup sour cream
> $^{1}/_{2}$ cup good mayonnaise
> 1 tablespoon kosher salt
> $1^{1}/_{2}$ teaspoons freshly ground black pepper
> 1 cup diced golden pineapple

Place the raisins in a small bowl and add enough hot tap water to cover. Set aside.

Fit a food processor with the coarsest grating disk. Wash the carrots and cut them to fit in the feed tube of the food processor lying on their sides. Grate all the carrots and put them in a large bowl. Sprinkle the carrots with the sugar and lemon juice.

In a smaller bowl, whisk together the sour cream, mayonnaise, salt, and pepper. Add the sauce and the pineapple to the carrots and toss well. Drain the raisins and add to the salad. Toss well. Cover with plastic wrap and refrigerate for an hour, if possible, to allow the flavors to blend. Add salt and lemon juice to taste and serve cold or at room temperature.

white pizzas with arugula

makes 6 pizzas

My television producer Rachel Purnell told me about having eaten a white pizza with arugula in London and I thought, "What a great idea!" I love the interplay of the hot, crisp pizza with the cold lemony arugula salad on top. I finish it with coarse sea salt just before serving. You'll need three sheet pans to bake all the pizzas at the same time.

FOR THE PIZZA

1¼ cups warm water (100 to 110 degrees)
2 packages dry yeast
1 tablespoon honey
Good olive oil
4 cups all-purpose flour, plus extra for kneading
Kosher salt
4 garlic cloves, sliced
5 sprigs fresh thyme
¼ teaspoon crushed red pepper flakes
Freshly ground black pepper
3 cups grated Italian Fontina cheese (8 ounces)
1½ cups grated fresh mozzarella (7 ounces)
11 ounces creamy goat cheese such as Montrachet, crumbled

FOR THE SALAD

½ cup good olive oil
¼ cup freshly squeezed lemon juice
8 ounces baby arugula

For the dough, combine the water, yeast, honey, and 3 tablespoons olive oil in the bowl of an electric mixer fitted with a dough hook. When the yeast is dissolved, add 3 cups of the flour, then 2 teaspoons salt, and mix on medium-low speed. While mixing, add up to 1 more cup of flour, or just enough to make a soft dough. Knead the dough for about 10 minutes until smooth, sprinkling it with the flour as necessary to keep it from sticking to the bowl. When the dough is ready, turn it out onto a floured board and knead it by hand a dozen times. It should be smooth and elastic. Place the dough in a well-oiled bowl and turn it to cover it lightly with oil. Cover the bowl with a kitchen towel and allow the dough to rise at room temperature for 30 minutes.

Meanwhile, make the garlic oil. Place ½ cup olive oil, the garlic, thyme, and red pepper flakes in a small saucepan and bring to a simmer over low heat. Cook for 10 minutes, making sure the garlic doesn't burn. Set aside.

Preheat the oven to 500 degrees. (Be sure your oven is clean!)

Dump the dough onto a board and divide it into 6 equal pieces. Place them on a sheet pan lined with parchment paper and cover them with a damp towel. Allow the dough to rest for 10 minutes. Use immediately, or refrigerate for up to 4 hours.

Press and stretch each ball into an 8-inch circle and place 2 circles on each parchment-lined sheet pan. (If you've chilled the dough, take it out of the refrigerator approximately 30 minutes ahead to let it come to room temperature.) Brush the pizzas with the garlic oil, and sprinkle each one liberally with salt and pepper. Sprinkle the pizzas evenly with Fontina, mozzarella, and goat cheese. Drizzle each pizza with 1 tablespoon more of the garlic oil and bake for 10 to 15 minutes, until the crusts are crisp and the cheeses begin to brown.

Meanwhile, for the vinaigrette, whisk together ½ cup of the olive oil, the lemon juice, 1 teaspoon salt, and ½ teaspoon pepper. When the pizzas are done, place the arugula in a large bowl and toss with just enough lemon vinaigrette to moisten. Place a large bunch of arugula on each pizza and serve immediately.

Garlic oil is also delicious in vinaigrettes or drizzled on vegetables.

Make sure the bowl is warm before you put the water and yeast in; the water must be warm for the yeast to develop.

creamy cucumber salad

serves 8

I love cucumbers, though not the traditional ones; even after they're peeled, I find them bitter. Cucumber salads are often dressed with sour cream, but using yogurt and the hothouse or "seedless" cucumbers you can now find in the grocery store makes this classic recipe lighter and sweeter. For me, this is a perfect summer salad to go with salmon for lunch or grilled chicken for dinner.

4 hothouse cucumbers, thinly sliced (3 to 4 pounds)

2 small red onions, thinly sliced in half rounds

Kosher salt

4 cups (32 ounces) plain whole-milk yogurt

1 cup (8 ounces) sour cream

2 tablespoons champagne vinegar or white wine vinegar

$1/2$ cup minced fresh dill

$1^1/2$ teaspoons freshly ground black pepper

Because hothouse cucumbers are not waxed they don't need to be peeled.

Mix the cucumbers, red onions, and $1^1/2$ tablespoons of salt in a bowl. Pour them into a colander and suspend it over a bowl. Wrap the bowl and colander with plastic wrap, and place in the refrigerator to drain for at least 4 hours or overnight. Discard the liquid that collects in the bowl.

Pour the yogurt into a sieve lined with a paper towel and suspend it over another bowl. Wrap the bowl and sieve in plastic wrap and refrigerate for at least 4 hours or overnight. Discard the liquid that collects in the second bowl.

When the cucumbers are ready, roll them up in paper towels or a kitchen towel and press the towel lightly to remove most of the liquid. Place the cucumbers and yogurt in a large bowl with the sour cream, vinegar, dill, 2 teaspoons salt, and the pepper. Toss well and refrigerate for a few hours to allow the flavors to blend. Sprinkle with $1/2$ teaspoon salt and $1/2$ teaspoon pepper and serve chilled.

warm goat cheese in phyllo

serves 6

I do love a warm goat cheese salad. Goat cheeses generally have half the fat of regular cheese, which makes this a light but very satisfying meal. You can certainly serve the cheese plain, but why not dress it up with a little phyllo dough to make it special?

12 sheets phyllo dough, defrosted

6 tablespoons (¾ stick) unsalted butter, melted

2 to 3 tablespoons plain dry bread crumbs

3 (3.5- to 5.5-ounce) fresh goat cheese discs (see note)

Baby salad greens, such as arugula and mesclun mix, for 6

FOR THE VINAIGRETTE

2 tablespoons champagne vinegar

1 teaspoon Dijon mustard

½ teaspoon minced garlic

1 teaspoon kosher salt

½ teaspoon freshly ground black pepper

½ cup good olive oil

I use Coach Farm (5.5-ounce) or Montrachet (3.5-ounce) goat cheese discs.

Preheat the oven to 375 degrees.

Unroll the sheets of phyllo dough on a flat surface and cover them with a slightly damp towel. (If the towel is too wet, the dough will get sticky.) Working quickly so the dough doesn't dry out, place one sheet of phyllo on a board, brush lightly with melted butter, and sprinkle lightly with bread crumbs. Place a second sheet of phyllo on top, brush with melted butter, and sprinkle with bread crumbs. Continue until you have 4 sheets stacked up. Cut the sheets in half crosswise to make 2 almost-squares.

Cut one of the goat cheeses in half horizontally, making 2 thin discs. Place each disc in the center of one phyllo square. Starting at one corner, fold the phyllo up over the cheese and continue folding and pleating the phyllo around the cheese, as though you're wrapping a round gift that's tied on top. You will end with extra phyllo dough on top; twist the excess into a top-knot. Brush the discs all over with melted butter and place on a sheet pan lined with parchment paper. Continue with the remaining phyllo dough and 2 goat cheese discs to make 4 additional packages.

Bake for 20 minutes, until the phyllo is lightly browned. Allow to cool for 5 minutes.

While the cheese packages bake, place the salad greens in a large bowl. Whisk the vinegar, mustard, garlic, salt, and pepper together in a small bowl. Still whisking, slowly add the olive oil, making an emulsion. Toss the salad greens with enough vinaigrette to moisten.

Distribute the salad among 6 plates and place one warm goat cheese package in the center of each plate. Sprinkle with salt and pepper and serve.

roasted butternut squash salad with warm cider vinaigrette

serves 4

My friend Stephen Drucker described a warm butternut squash salad that he'd been served and asked if I could make one. Why not? I love the interplay of hot and cold plus the sweet butternut squash, tart dried cranberries, nutty Parmesan, and bitter arugula.

1 (1½-pound) butternut squash, peeled and ¾-inch diced
Good olive oil
1 tablespoon pure maple syrup
Kosher salt and freshly ground black pepper
3 tablespoons dried cranberries
¾ cup apple cider or apple juice
2 tablespoons cider vinegar
2 tablespoons minced shallots
2 teaspoons Dijon mustard
4 ounces baby arugula, washed and spun dry
½ cup walnut halves, toasted (page 78)
¾ cup freshly grated Parmesan cheese (see note)

Preheat the oven to 400 degrees.

Place the squash on a sheet pan. Add 2 tablespoons olive oil, the maple syrup, 1 teaspoon salt, and ½ teaspoon pepper and toss. Roast the squash for 15 to 20 minutes, turning once, until tender. Add the cranberries to the pan for the last 5 minutes.

While the squash is roasting, combine the apple cider, vinegar, and shallots in a small saucepan and bring to a boil over medium-high heat. Cook for 6 to 8 minutes, until the cider is reduced to about ¼ cup. Off the heat, whisk in the mustard, ½ cup olive oil, 1 teaspoon salt, and ½ teaspoon pepper.

Place the arugula in a large salad bowl and add the roasted squash mixture, the walnuts, and the grated Parmesan. Spoon just enough vinaigrette over the salad to moisten, and toss well. Sprinkle with salt and pepper and serve immediately.

For this salad, I grate the Parmesan on a box grater as I would grate carrots.

roasted tomato caprese salad

serves 6

I love tomatoes but they're usually only good in summer when I can get them at a farmstand. I discovered that if you slow-roast the plum tomatoes that you can find all year long at the grocery store, they will have full, rich summer tomato flavor. Now I can make Caprese salad whenever I want.

12 plum tomatoes, halved lengthwise, seeds (not cores) removed

¼ cup good olive oil, plus more for drizzling

1½ tablespoons balsamic vinegar

2 large garlic cloves, minced

2 teaspoons sugar

Kosher salt and freshly ground black pepper

16 ounces fresh salted mozzarella

12 fresh basil leaves, julienned

Preheat the oven to 275 degrees.

Arrange the tomatoes on a sheet pan, cut sides up, in a single layer. Drizzle with the olive oil and balsamic vinegar. Sprinkle with the garlic, sugar, 1½ teaspoons salt, and ½ teaspoon pepper. Roast for 2 hours until the tomatoes are concentrated and begin to caramelize. Allow the tomatoes to cool to room temperature.

Cut the mozzarella into slices slightly less than ½ inch thick. If the slices of mozzarella are larger than the tomatoes, cut the mozzarella slices in half. Layer the tomatoes alternately with the mozzarella on a platter and scatter the basil on top. Sprinkle lightly with salt and pepper and drizzle lightly with olive oil. Serve at room temperature.

tomato & goat cheese tarts

makes 4 individual tarts

I've been in the food business for thirty years and I've made thousands of pies and tarts, but I have to admit that pastry still makes me anxious. When I discovered frozen puff pastry, it was such a relief. This is an elegant lunch or a substantial first course for a dinner party.

 1 package (17.3 ounces/2 sheets) puff pastry, defrosted
 Good olive oil
 4 cups thinly sliced yellow onions (2 large onions)
 3 large garlic cloves, cut into thin slivers
 Kosher salt and freshly ground black pepper
 3 tablespoons dry white wine
 2 teaspoons minced fresh thyme leaves
 4 tablespoons freshly grated Parmesan cheese
 4 ounces garlic-and-herb goat cheese, such as Montrachet
 1 large tomato, cut into 4 (^{1}/$_4$-inch-thick) slices
 3 tablespoons julienned basil leaves
 2 ounces Parmesan cheese, shaved with a vegetable peeler

Unfold a sheet of puff pastry on a lightly floured surface and roll it lightly to an 11 × 11-inch square. Using a 6-inch-wide saucer or other round object as a guide, cut 2 circles from the sheet of puff pastry, discarding the scraps. Repeat with the second pastry sheet to make 4 circles in all. Place the pastry circles on 2 sheet pans lined with parchment paper and refrigerate until ready to use.

Preheat the oven to 425 degrees.

Heat 3 tablespoons of olive oil in a large skillet over medium to low heat and add the onions and garlic. Sauté for 15 to 20 minutes, stirring frequently, until the onions are limp and there is almost no moisture remaining in the skillet. Add ^{1}/$_2$ teaspoon salt, ^{1}/$_4$ teaspoon pepper, the wine, and thyme and continue to cook for another 10 minutes, until the onions are lightly browned. Remove from the heat.

Using a sharp paring knife, score a ^{1}/$_4$-inch-wide border around each pastry circle. Prick the pastry inside the score lines with the tines of a fork and sprinkle a tablespoon of grated Parmesan on each round, staying inside the scored border.

Place one-quarter of the onion mixture on each circle, again staying within the scored edge. Crumble 1 ounce of the goat cheese on top of the onions. Place a slice of tomato in the center of each tart. Brush the tomato lightly with olive oil and sprinkle with basil, salt, and pepper. Finally, scatter 4 or 5 shards of Parmesan on each tart.

Bake for 20 to 25 minutes, until the pastry is golden brown. The bottom sheet pan may need an extra few minutes in the oven. Serve hot or warm.

truffled filet of beef sandwiches

serves 6

I love to take something ordinary and make it really special and that's just what I've done here. This isn't your average roast beef sandwich; it's filet of beef with black truffle butter, Parmesan cheese, and bitter arugula. Your friends will swoon.

1½ to 2 pounds filet of beef, trimmed and tied
1 tablespoon unsalted butter, at room temperature
    Kosher salt and coarsely ground black pepper
2 French baguettes, 18 to 20 inches long
3 ounces black truffle butter, at room temperature (see note)
1 (2-ounce) chunk good Parmesan cheese
    Fresh baby arugula

Ask your butcher to trim and tie the filet of beef for you.

Dartagnan.com sells black and white truffle butter in 3-ounce packages. They're surprisingly inexpensive; I order a few at a time and keep them in the freezer.

Preheat the oven to 500 degrees. (Be sure your oven is very clean!)

Place the beef on a sheet pan and pat the outside dry with a paper towel. Spread the unsalted butter all over the beef with your hands. Sprinkle the beef evenly with 1½ teaspoons salt and 1½ teaspoons pepper. Roast for exactly 22 minutes for rare and 25 minutes for medium-rare.

Remove the beef from the oven, cover it tightly with aluminum foil, and allow it to rest at room temperature for 15 minutes. Remove the strings and slice the filet about ¼ inch thick.

Split the baguettes lengthwise but not all the way through. Spread the bottom halves generously with the truffle butter. Top with a layer of sliced beef and sprinkle with salt and pepper.

Using a vegetable peeler, shave the Parmesan into thin shards and scatter the shards over the sliced beef on each sandwich. Finish with a sprinkling of arugula leaves. Fold the tops of the sandwiches over, cut each baguette diagonally into 3 or 4 sandwiches, and serve right away.

roasted pears with blue cheese

serves 6

In the autumn when pears are delicious, I bake them with some crumbled blue cheese and serve it with a good arugula salad. It's light but so satisfying.

3 ripe but firm Anjou pears

Freshly squeezed lemon juice (3 lemons)

3 ounces coarsely crumbled sharp blue cheese such as Stilton

¼ cup dried cranberries

¼ cup walnut halves, toasted (page 78) and chopped

½ cup apple cider

3 tablespoons port

⅓ cup light brown sugar, lightly packed

¼ cup good olive oil

6 ounces baby arugula

Kosher salt

Preheat the oven to 375 degrees.

Peel the pears and slice them lengthwise into halves. With a small, sharp paring knife and a melon baller, remove the core and seeds from each pear, leaving a round well for the filling. Trim a small slice away from the rounded sides of each pear half so that they will sit in the baking dish without wobbling. Toss the pears with lemon juice to prevent them from turning brown. Arrange them, core side up, in a baking dish large enough to hold the pears snugly.

Gently toss the crumbled blue cheese, dried cranberries, and walnuts together in a small bowl. Divide the mixture among the pears, mounding it on top of the indentation.

In the same small bowl, combine the apple cider, port, and brown sugar, stirring to dissolve the sugar. Pour the mixture over and around the pears. Bake the pears, basting occasionally with the cider mixture, for 30 minutes, or until tender. Set aside until warm or at room temperature.

Just before serving, whisk together the olive oil, $^1/_4$ cup lemon juice, and $^1/_4$ cup of the basting liquid in a large bowl. Add the arugula and toss well. Divide the arugula among 6 plates and top each with a pear half. Drizzle each pear with some of the basting liquid, sprinkle with salt, and serve.

mâche with warm brie & apples

serves 4

Mâche is a specialty lettuce that is also called lamb's lettuce or corn salad because it grows wild in cornfields. It's delicate and has a slightly nutty flavor that works well with the warm, gooey Brie and crisp apples. It usually comes with roots attached. Remove the roots and growing soil, wash it well, and then spin it dry.

1 French baguette, sliced ½ inch thick diagonally
12 ounces good French Brie, cut into 4 wedges
6 tablespoons honey
3 tablespoons roasted and salted pistachios (see note)
4 ounces mâche leaves (8 to 10 ounces with roots attached)
1 tablespoon syrupy aged balsamic vinegar
3 tablespoons good olive oil
   Kosher salt and freshly ground black pepper
1 large Granny Smith apple, cored and thinly sliced

For 3 tablespoons of pistachios, you'll need 2 ounces shelled pistachios or 4 ounces in the shell.

Preheat the oven to 350 degrees. Place the sliced bread on a sheet pan and bake for 6 to 8 minutes, until crisp.

Arrange the 4 wedges of Brie snugly in one layer in a glass or ceramic baking dish. Drizzle the honey over the wedges and then scatter the pistachios over the top. Bake for 3 to 5 minutes (depending on the ripeness of the Brie) until the Brie just begins to ooze but isn't melted. Be careful—it happens fast!

Place the mâche in a large bowl and toss it gently with the balsamic vinegar and olive oil. Sprinkle with salt and pepper. Divide the salad among 4 large salad plates and place a piece of the warm Brie with the pistachios in the center of each plate. Place a quarter of the apple slices on each plate fanned out on one side of the Brie. Place 2 or 3 slices of toasted baguette on the other side of the Brie and sprinkle generously with salt and pepper. Drizzle with the honey still in the baking dish and serve immediately.

dinner

tuscan lemon chicken

roasted turkey roulade

chicken bouillabaisse

coq au vin

company pot roast

niman ranch burgers

french bistro steaks

parker's beef stew

herb-marinated loin of pork

baked shrimp scampi

easy sole meunière

bay scallop gratins

indonesian grilled swordfish

mustard-roasted fish

soft-shell crab sandwiches

prosciutto roasted bass

pasta with pecorino & pepper

wild mushroom risotto

spring green risotto

dinner spanakopitas

tagliarelle with truffle butter

10 things *not* to serve at a dinner party

1 Appetizers that take two hands. You're holding a cocktail having a perfectly nice conversation and someone offers you a grilled scallop served in a martini glass. Now, what exactly are you supposed to do with your drink ? I'd pass it up.

2 Beets or red wine. If you're serving buffet style and eating dinner on your lap in the living room, you're just inviting disaster.

3 Three rich courses. It's important to balance the courses, so if you're serving a rich main course, start with a green salad and end with baked fruit and a delicious cookie. Your friends will thank you.

4 Nuts. Many people hate nuts or are allergic to them. Unless I know my guests well, I avoid dishes with nuts.

5 Garlic and raw onions. Now, I like chicken with forty cloves of garlic as much as the next guy, but I have to know the other guests *very* well to want to talk to them knowing I have garlic breath.

6 Spinach and poppy seeds. How many times have you been talking to someone you barely know who has spinach between their front teeth? Avoid embarrasment and serve something else.

7 Corn on the cob. Same problem as spinach. If I serve corn, I cut it off the cob, sauté it with some butter, salt, and pepper, and serve it in a big bowl. No dental floss required.

8 Two fish courses. Most people eat meat but fewer eat fish and seafood. If I'm serving smoked salmon to start, I'm always sure to have a traditional chicken or filet of beef for dinner.

9 Offal. If your family loves liver and bacon—great. Make it for them. But don't spring it on unsuspecting dinner guests without checking first.

10 Raw beef or raw eggs. I never eat steak tartare or raw eggs, unless I know they're from a safe place, so I'm not about to serve food to friends that requires me to explain its provenance.

tuscan lemon chicken

serves 2 or 3

The Palm restaurant in East Hampton makes a delicious Tuscan chicken that we order all the time. When I decided to make something similar at home, I found how delicious it was to grill some lemon halves and squeeze them onto the chicken. Don't skimp on the salt; it brings out all the flavors.

1 (3½-pound) chicken, flattened (see note)
  Kosher salt
⅓ cup good olive oil
2 teaspoons grated lemon zest (2 lemons)
⅓ cup freshly squeezed lemon juice
1 tablespoon minced garlic (3 cloves)
1 tablespoon minced fresh rosemary leaves
  Freshly ground black pepper
1 lemon, halved

Stand the chicken upright and cut out the backbone with a large kitchen knife. Spread the chicken open on a board with the skin side down. Cut around and remove the breastbone with a boning knife. (You can ask your butcher to do all of this for you.)

If you want to use the leftover marinade as a sauce, put it in a small saucepan and simmer it over low heat for 5 minutes.

Sprinkle the chicken with 1 teaspoon salt on each side.

Combine the olive oil, lemon zest, lemon juice, garlic, rosemary, and 1 teaspoon pepper in a ceramic or glass dish just large enough to hold the flattened chicken. Add the chicken, and turn to coat. Cover the dish with plastic wrap and refrigerate for at least 4 hours or overnight, turning once or twice.

When ready to grill, prepare a hot charcoal fire on one side of a grill (or turn a gas grill on low heat). Spread ¼ of the coals across the other side of the grill. Place the chicken on the cooler side skin side up, and weight it down with the dish you used for marinating. Cook for 12 to 15 minutes, until the underside is golden brown. Turn the chicken skin side down, weight again with the dish, and cook for another 12 to 15 minutes, until the skin is golden brown and the chicken is cooked through. Place the lemon halves on the cool side of the grill, cut side down, for the last 10 minutes of cooking. Remove the chicken to a plate or cutting board, cover with aluminum foil, and allow to rest for 5 minutes. Cut the chicken in quarters, sprinkle with salt, and serve with the grilled lemon halves.

roasted turkey roulade

serves 6 or 7

I don't know anyone who looks forward to carving a turkey on Thanksgiving. You're at the table, everyone's watching, and you're struggling to carve a hot bird. Instead, I decided to make a roasted turkey breast stuffed with all kinds of delicious things—sausage, cranberries, and figs. No bones and it cooks to juicy perfection in under two hours. How easy is that?

3/4 cup large-diced dried figs, stems removed

3/4 cup dried cranberries

1/2 cup Calvados or brandy

4 tablespoons (1/2 stick) unsalted butter

1 1/2 cups diced onions (2 onions)

1 cup (1/2-inch-diced) celery (3 stalks)

3/4 pound pork sausage, casings removed (sweet and hot mixed)

1 1/2 tablespoons chopped fresh rosemary leaves

3 tablespoons pine nuts, toasted (page 43)

3 cups Pepperidge Farm herb-seasoned stuffing mix

1 1/2 cups chicken stock, preferably homemade (page 61)

1 extra-large egg, beaten

Kosher salt and freshly ground black pepper

1 whole (2 halves) turkey breast, boned and butterflied (5 pounds)

3 tablespoons unsalted butter, melted

Place the dried figs and cranberries in a small saucepan and pour in the Calvados and 1/2 cup water. Bring the mixture to a boil over medium heat, then lower the heat and simmer for 2 minutes. Remove from the heat and set aside.

Meanwhile, melt the butter in a large (12-inch) skillet over medium heat. Add the onions and celery and sauté until softened, about 5 minutes. Add the sausage, crumbling it into small bits with a fork, and sauté, stirring frequently, for 10 minutes, until

(recipe continues)

cooked and browned. Add the figs and cranberries with the liquid, the chopped rosemary, and pine nuts, and cook for 2 more minutes. Scrape up the brown bits with a wooden spoon.

Place the stuffing mix in a large bowl. Add the sausage mixture, chicken stock, egg, 1 teaspoon salt, and 1/2 teaspoon pepper and stir well. (The stuffing may be prepared ahead and stored in the refrigerator overnight.)

Preheat the oven to 325 degrees. Place a baking rack on a sheet pan.

If you want to serve this with gravy, you can find a delicious recipe on page 119 in Barefoot Contessa Family Style.

Lay the butterflied turkey breast skin side down on a cutting board. Sprinkle the meat with 2 teaspoons salt and 1 teaspoon pepper. Spread the stuffing in a 1/2-inch-thick layer over the meat, leaving a half-inch border on all sides. Don't mound the stuffing or the turkey will be difficult to roll. (Place the leftover stuffing in a buttered gratin dish and bake for the last 45 minutes of roasting alongside the turkey.) Starting at one end, roll the turkey like a jelly roll and tuck in any stuffing that tries to escape on the sides. Tie the roast firmly with kitchen twine every 2 inches to make a compact cylinder.

Place the stuffed turkey breast seam side down on the rack on the sheet pan. Brush with the melted butter, sprinkle generously with salt and pepper, and roast for 1 3/4 to 2 hours, until a thermometer reads 150 degrees in the center. (I test in a few places.) Cover the turkey with aluminum foil and allow it to rest at room temperature for 15 minutes. Carve 1/2-inch-thick slices and serve warm with the extra stuffing.

chicken bouillabaisse

serves 3

Years ago when I first got into the food business, I took classes with a wonderful teacher in New York named Lydie Marshall. She was originally from Provence and many of her recipes had a Provençal theme. I've always remembered a chicken bouillabaisse that she made, so I wanted to make one like it. This is basically a chicken stew with garlicky rouille served on top. On a cold winter night, it will warm your bones.

1 (4- to 5-pound) chicken, cut into 8 to 10 pieces (see note)
Kosher salt and freshly ground black pepper
1 tablespoon minced fresh rosemary leaves
Good olive oil
1 large head garlic, separated into cloves and peeled
1 teaspoon saffron threads
1 teaspoon whole fennel seeds
1 (15-ounce) can tomato purée
1½ cups chicken stock, preferably homemade (page 61)
1 cup dry white wine
3 tablespoons Pernod
1 pound baby Yukon Gold potatoes, halved
Rouille, for serving (recipe follows)
Crusty French bread, for serving

Ask the butcher to cut the chicken into eight serving pieces and, if the breasts are large, cut them in half crosswise.

Pat the chicken dry with paper towels and season it generously with salt, pepper, and the rosemary. Heat 2 tablespoons of olive oil over medium heat in a large Dutch oven and brown the chicken pieces in batches until nicely browned all over, about 5 to 7 minutes per batch. Transfer the browned chicken pieces to a plate and set aside.

Lower the heat to medium-low and add the garlic, saffron, fennel seeds, tomato purée, chicken stock, white wine, Pernod, 2 teaspoons salt, and 1 teaspoon pepper to the pot. Stir and scrape

(recipe continues)

To finish, you could add a dash of Pernod if you want more fennel flavor or a splash of white wine if it needs a little alcohol edge. A sprinkling of salt is good, too.

up any browned bits on the bottom, and simmer for 30 to 40 minutes, until the garlic is very tender, stirring occasionally.

Meanwhile, preheat the oven to 300 degrees.

Carefully pour the sauce into the bowl of a food processor fitted with the steel blade. Purée until smooth. Return the sauce to the Dutch oven and add the potatoes and browned chicken pieces with their juices. Stir carefully.

Cover the pot and bake for 45 to 55 minutes, until the potatoes are tender and the chicken is done. Check the seasonings and serve hot in shallow bowls with big dollops of rouille and slices of crusty bread.

rouille makes 1 cup

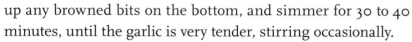

  4 **large garlic cloves**
1½ **teaspoons kosher salt**
  1 **extra-large egg yolk, at room temperature**
1½ **tablespoons freshly squeezed lemon juice**
 ½ **teaspoon saffron threads**
 ¼ **teaspoon crushed red pepper flakes**
  1 **cup good olive oil**

A dollop of this garlicky mayonnaise gives any dish a Provençal flavor.

Place the garlic and salt on a cutting board and mince together. Transfer the mixture to a food processor fitted with the steel blade. Add the egg yolk, lemon juice, saffron, and red pepper flakes. Process until smooth.

With the machine running, pour the olive oil in a thin, steady stream through the feed tube to make a thick mayonnaise emulsion. Transfer the rouille to a serving bowl and store it in the refrigerator until ready to serve.

coq au vin

serves 6

Over the years I've tried many times to make a good coq au vin, the renowned French chicken stew with red wine, but with disappointing results. My television producer Olivia Grove one day told me, "Well, it's just beef bourguignon with chicken," and I thought, "So it is!" With that in mind, I adapted my old recipe for beef and came up with an easy chicken version that's such a satisfying winter dinner. Usually the chicken cooks for hours and is dry and stringy, but I found that after only thirty to forty minutes in the oven, the chicken is perfectly cooked and still tender and juicy.

 Good olive oil
8 ounces good bacon or pancetta, diced
2 (3- to 4-pound) chickens, each cut into 8 serving pieces
 Kosher salt and freshly ground black pepper
1 pound carrots, cut diagonally into 1-inch pieces
2 yellow onions, sliced
2 teaspoons chopped garlic (2 cloves)
¼ cup Cognac or good brandy
1 (750-ml) bottle good dry red wine such as Burgundy
2 cups chicken stock, preferably homemade (page 61)
1 bunch fresh thyme sprigs
4 tablespoons (½ stick) unsalted butter, at room temperature, divided
3 tablespoons all-purpose flour
1 pound frozen small whole onions
1 pound porcini or cremini mushrooms, stems removed and thickly sliced

Preheat the oven to 275 degrees.

Heat 1 tablespoon olive oil in a large Dutch oven over medium heat. Add the bacon and cook for 8 to 10 minutes, until lightly browned. Remove the bacon to a plate with a slotted spoon.

(recipe continues)

Meanwhile, pat the chicken dry with paper towels. Liberally sprinkle the chicken on both sides with salt and pepper. After the bacon is removed, add a few of the chicken pieces in a single layer and brown for about 5 minutes, turning to brown evenly. Remove the chicken pieces to the plate with the bacon and continue to add the chicken in batches until all the chicken is browned. Set aside.

Add the carrots, onions, 1 tablespoon salt, and 2 teaspoons pepper to the pot and cook over medium heat for 10 to 12 minutes, stirring occasionally, until the onions are lightly browned. Add the garlic and cook for 1 more minute. Add the Cognac, *stand back!,* and carefully ignite with a match to burn off the alcohol. Put the bacon, chicken, and any juices that collect on the plate into the pot. Add the wine, chicken stock, and thyme sprigs and bring to a boil. Cover the pot with a tight-fitting lid and place in the oven for 30 to 40 minutes, until the chicken is just no longer pink. Remove from the oven and place on top of the stove.

A splash of red wine or Cognac at the end brings up the rich flavor in the sauce.

Mash 2 tablespoons of the butter and the flour together in a small bowl and stir the paste into the stew. Add the frozen onions. In a medium sauté pan, melt the remaining 2 tablespoons butter and cook the mushrooms over medium-low heat for 5 to 10 minutes, until browned. Add to the stew. Bring the stew to a simmer and cook for another 10 minutes. Season to taste. Serve hot.

company pot roast

serves 8

Most pot roast recipes recommend that you strain the vegetables to make the sauce, which makes it too thin for my taste. If you don't strain the vegetables, though, the sauce is too chunky. I got the best of both worlds by puréeing half the sauce and pouring it back into the pot with the chunky half. This recipe makes a lot of sauce, but if there are leftovers, it's delicious the next day on pasta. A splash of red wine in the pot before serving gives the sauce a nice edge.

1 (4- to 5-pound) prime boneless beef chuck roast, tied
   Kosher salt and freshly ground black pepper
   All-purpose flour
   Good olive oil
2 cups chopped carrots (4 carrots)
2 cups chopped yellow onions (2 onions)
2 cups chopped celery (4 stalks)
2 cups chopped leeks, white and light green parts
   (2 to 4 leeks)
5 large garlic cloves, peeled and crushed
2 cups good red wine, such as Burgundy
2 tablespoons Cognac or brandy
1 (28-ounce) can whole plum tomatoes in purée
1 cup chicken stock, preferably homemade (page 61)
1 chicken bouillon cube
3 branches fresh thyme
2 branches fresh rosemary
1 tablespoon unsalted butter, at room temperature

Preheat the oven to 325 degrees.

Pat the beef dry with a paper towel. Season the roast all over with 1 tablespoon salt and 1½ teaspoons pepper. Dredge the whole roast in flour, including the ends. In a large Dutch oven, heat

(recipe continues)

2 tablespoons olive oil over medium heat. Add the roast and sear for 4 to 5 minutes, until nicely browned. Turn and sear the other side and then turn and sear the ends. This should take 4 to 5 minutes for each side. Remove the roast to a large plate.

Add 2 tablespoons olive oil to the Dutch oven. Add the carrots, onions, celery, leeks, garlic, 1 tablespoon salt, and 1½ teaspoons pepper and cook over medium heat for 10 to 15 minutes, stirring occasionally, until tender but not browned. Add the wine and Cognac and bring to a boil. Add the tomatoes, chicken stock, bouillon cube, 2 teaspoons salt, and 1 teaspoon pepper. Tie the thyme and rosemary together with kitchen string and add to the pot. Put the roast back into the pot, bring to a boil, and cover. Place in the oven for 2½ hours, until the meat is fork tender or about 160 degrees internally. Turn the heat down to 250 degrees after about an hour to keep the sauce at a simmer.

Remove the roast to a cutting board. Remove the herb bundle and discard. Skim off as much fat as possible from the sauce. Transfer half the sauce and vegetables to a blender or a food processor fitted with the steel blade and purée until smooth. Pour the purée back into the pot, place on the stovetop over low heat, and return the sauce to a simmer. Place 2 tablespoons flour and the butter in a small bowl and mash them together with a fork. Stir into the sauce and simmer for 2 minutes, stirring until thickened. Taste for seasonings. Remove the strings from the roast, and slice the meat. Serve warm with the sauce spooned over it.

niman ranch burgers

serves 6

Niman Ranch produces the most delicious beef; their cattle are all natu-rally grown and primarily grass-fed. You can find it at your local butcher shop or order it at nimanranch.com. These hamburgers with caramelized onions are a classic American dish with the volume turned way up.

- 2 pounds ground Niman Ranch beef or other grass-fed premium beef (80% lean and 20% fat)
- 1 tablespoon good Dijon mustard
- 3 tablespoons good olive oil, plus extra for brushing the grill
- 1 teaspoon kosher salt
- 1 teaspoon freshly ground black pepper
- 3 sandwich-size English muffins, halved
  Good mayonnaise
  Caramelized Onions (recipe follows)

Build a charcoal fire or heat a gas grill.

Place the ground beef in a large bowl and add the mustard, olive oil, salt, and pepper. Mix gently with a fork to combine, taking care not to compress the ingredients. Shape the meat into 6 (3^1/$_2$-inch) patties of equal size and thickness.

When the grill is medium-hot, brush the grill grate with oil to keep the burgers from sticking. Place the burgers on the grill and cook for 4 minutes. Using a big spatula, turn the burgers and cook for another 3 to 4 minutes, until medium-rare, or cook longer if you prefer hamburgers more well done.

Meanwhile, break apart the English muffins and toast the 6 halves cut side down on the grill. Spread each half with mayon-naise and top with a burger and then with a heaping tablespoon of caramelized onions. Serve hot.

caramelized onions

serves 6

When my friend Ayyam Sarreau asked her grandmother how to cook onions, she said, "Turn your back on them." What great advice! Caramelizing the onions gives them such a sweet flavor, and the splash of sherry vinegar balances the sweetness of the onions with a little vinegary bite. This is perfect served on hamburgers or with a simple grilled veal chop.

- 2 tablespoons good olive oil
- 2 tablespoons unsalted butter
- 2 pounds yellow onions, peeled and sliced in half-rounds
- $1/2$ teaspoon fresh thyme leaves
- 2 tablespoons sherry wine vinegar
- 1 teaspoon kosher salt
- $1/2$ teaspoon freshly ground black pepper

Heat the olive oil and butter in a large shallow pot, add the onions and thyme, and toss with the oil. Place the lid on top and cook over medium-low heat for about 10 minutes to sweat the onions. Remove the lid and continue to cook over medium-low heat, stirring occasionally, for 25 to 30 minutes, until the onions are caramelized and golden brown. If the onions are cooking too fast, lower the heat. Add the vinegar, salt, and pepper and cook for 2 more minutes, scraping the brown bits from the pan. Season to taste (they should be very highly seasoned).

french bistro steaks with provençal butter

serves 4 to 6

One of my favorite meals in France is a simple cut of steak called onglet *and you find it in many bistros. Here it's called hanger steak; it's a little less tender than other cuts but it has lots of flavor. This is a dish to please any man—a nice grilled steak with butter flavored with garlic, capers, and chives. Yum. And if you insisted on serving it with a big pile of Matchstick Potatoes* (Barefoot in Paris, *page 153*), *I'm sure no one would object.*

The Provençal butter can be stored in the refrigerator for a few days or in the freezer for a few months.

1 large garlic clove, minced
4 anchovy fillets, drained and chopped
1 tablespoon capers, drained
2 tablespoons minced fresh chives
1 teaspoon fresh thyme leaves
1 teaspoon grated lemon zest
½ teaspoon freshly ground black pepper
6 tablespoons (¾ stick) unsalted butter at room temperature
4 hanger steaks, 8 to 10 ounces each
4 tablespoons good olive oil
4 teaspoons herbes de Provence
Kosher salt and coarsely cracked black pepper

For the Provençal butter, place the garlic, anchovies, capers, chives, thyme, lemon zest, and pepper in a food processor and pulse the machine a few times to combine. Add the butter and process briefly to combine the ingredients. Place the butter mixture on a piece of parchment or wax paper and roll it into a log 1½ inches in diameter and 5 inches long, twisting the ends. Store the butter in the refrigerator.

Heat a gas or charcoal grill.

Place the hanger steaks on a platter and drizzle each one with 1 tablespoon of the olive oil. Sprinkle each steak with 1 teaspoon of the herbes de Provence and season generously with salt and pepper. Set aside at room temperature for 10 to 15 minutes.

When the grill is hot, grill the steaks for 4 to 5 minutes on each side, turning once, for medium-rare. Place the steaks on a platter, cover tightly with aluminum foil, and allow to rest for 15 minutes. Slice the steaks crosswise diagonally and serve hot with one or two slices of Provençal butter on top.

parker's beef stew

serves 6

Parker Hodges was the wonderful chef at my store, Barefoot Contessa. He grew up in Nicaragua and had no formal training as a cook, but good food is in his DNA. By marinating the beef overnight in red wine, he gave a simple cut of beef like chuck so much flavor. I make it days in advance and then reheat it for dinner with a chunk of French bread and a glass of wine.

If the stew is too thick, add a little more beef stock or water.

2½ pounds good-quality chuck beef, cut into 1¼-inch cubes

1 (750-ml) bottle good red wine, such as Cabernet Sauvignon

3 whole garlic cloves, smashed

3 bay leaves

6 ounces bacon, cut into 1-inch pieces

2 cups plus 2 tablespoons all-purpose flour
   Kosher salt and freshly ground black pepper

2 cups chopped yellow onions (2 onions)
   Good olive oil

2 tablespoons minced garlic (6 cloves)

1 pound carrots, peeled and cut diagonally into 1½-inch chunks

1 pound small potatoes, halved or quartered

1 (14½-ounce) can beef stock

1 large branch fresh rosemary

½ cup sun-dried tomatoes in oil, drained and sliced

2 tablespoons Worcestershire sauce

1 (10-ounce) package frozen peas (not petit pois)

Place the beef in a bowl with the red wine, garlic cloves, and bay leaves. Cover the bowl and marinate the beef in the refrigerator overnight.

Brown the bacon in a large (12-inch) sauté pan for 5 to 7 minutes, over medium-low heat. With a slotted spoon, transfer the bacon to a Dutch oven. Combine 2 cups of the flour, 1 tablespoon salt, and 1 tablespoon pepper in a bowl. Lift the beef out of the marinade and discard the bay leaves and garlic, saving the marinade. In batches, dredge the beef cubes in the flour mixture and then shake off the excess. In the same sauté pan, brown half the beef over medium heat for 5 to 7 minutes, turning to brown on all sides. Place the browned beef in the Dutch oven with the bacon and brown the remaining beef. Add the second batch to the Dutch oven.

Meanwhile, preheat the oven to 300 degrees.

Lower the heat under the sauté pan to medium-low, add the onions, and cook for 5 minutes, adding olive oil if necessary. Add the minced garlic and cook for 1 more minute. Add the carrots and potatoes and cook for 5 more minutes, stirring occasionally. Place all the vegetables in the Dutch oven with the beef. Add 2¹/₂ cups of the reserved marinade (discard the rest) to the sauté pan and cook over high heat to deglaze the bottom of the pan, scraping up all the brown bits with a wooden spoon. Add the beef stock, rosemary, sun-dried tomatoes, Worcestershire sauce, 1 tablespoon salt, and 2 teaspoons pepper. Pour the sauce over the meat and vegetables in the Dutch oven and bring it to a simmer over medium heat. Cover the pot and place it in the oven for 2 hours, until the meat and vegetables are all tender, stirring once during cooking. If the stew is boiling rather than simmering, lower the heat to 275 degrees.

When the stew is done and the meat is tender, discard the rosemary branch. Ladle 1 cup of the pan juices into a bowl and whisk in the remaining 2 tablespoons of flour. Pour it back into the stew, stir gently, and simmer for 3 minutes, until thickened. Stir in the frozen peas, season to taste, and serve hot.

herb-marinated loin of pork

serves 6

Pork tenderloins make a really quick dinner. I marinate them overnight in a mixture of lemon and herbs and then throw them on the grill for about twenty minutes. How easy is that?

Grated zest of 1 lemon
³/₄ cup freshly squeezed lemon juice (4 to 6 lemons)
¹/₂ cup good olive oil, plus extra for brushing the grill
2 tablespoons minced garlic (6 cloves)
1¹/₂ tablespoons minced fresh rosemary leaves
1 tablespoon chopped fresh thyme leaves
2 teaspoons Dijon mustard
Kosher salt
3 pork tenderloins (about 1 pound each)
Freshly ground black pepper

A plastic bag might not be elegant but it ensures that the meat is fully surrounded by the flavorful marinade.

When testing the meat temperature, stick an instant-read thermometer into the thicker end of the tenderloin as close to the center as possible.

Combine the lemon zest, lemon juice, olive oil, garlic, rosemary, thyme, mustard, and 2 teaspoons salt in a sturdy 1-gallon resealable plastic bag. Add the pork tenderloins and turn to coat with the marinade. Squeeze out the air and seal the bag. Marinate the pork in the refrigerator for at least 3 hours but preferably overnight.

When you're ready to cook, build a charcoal fire or heat a gas grill. Brush the cooking grate with oil to prevent the pork from sticking. Remove the tenderloins from the marinade and discard the marinade but leave the herbs that cling to the meat. Sprinkle the tenderloins generously with salt and pepper. Grill the tenderloins, turning a few times to brown on all sides, for 15 to 25 minutes (depending on the heat of the coals) until the meat registers 137 degrees at the thickest part. Transfer the tenderloins to a platter and cover tightly with aluminum foil. Allow to rest for 10 minutes. Carve in ¹/₂-inch-thick diagonal slices. The thickest part of the tenderloin will be quite pink (it's just fine!) and the thinnest part will be well done. Season with salt and pepper and serve warm, or at room temperature with the juices that collect in the platter.

baked shrimp scampi

serves 6

I'm always looking for dishes that I can prepare ahead of time and then bake just before dinner. This has all the wonderful flavor of shrimp scampi, but the crunchy crust makes it so much more interesting. A squeeze of fresh lemon juice before serving gives it a perfect hit of acidity to balance the richness of all that garlic and butter. This is one of Jeffrey's favorite dinners.

Butterflied shrimp means they're cut around the outer curve and opened like a book. Cut each shrimp deeply enough to open but not to cut in half.

Panko is available in the Asian section of the grocery store.

2 pounds (12 to 15 per pound) shrimp in the shell
3 tablespoons good olive oil
2 tablespoons dry white wine
  Kosher salt and freshly ground black pepper
12 tablespoons (1½ sticks) unsalted butter, at room temperature
4 teaspoons minced garlic (4 cloves)
¼ cup minced shallots
3 tablespoons minced fresh parsley
1 teaspoon minced fresh rosemary leaves
¼ teaspoon crushed red pepper flakes
1 teaspoon grated lemon zest
2 tablespoons freshly squeezed lemon juice
1 extra-large egg yolk
⅔ cup panko (Japanese dried bread flakes)
  Lemon wedges, for serving

Preheat the oven to 425 degrees.

Peel, devein, and butterfly the shrimp (see note), leaving the tails on. Place the shrimp in a mixing bowl and toss gently with the olive oil, wine, 2 teaspoons salt, and 1 teaspoon pepper. Allow to sit at room temperature while you make the butter and garlic mixture.

In a small bowl, mash the softened butter with the garlic, shallots, parsley, rosemary, red pepper flakes, lemon zest, lemon juice, egg yolk, panko, ½ teaspoon salt, and ¼ teaspoon pepper until combined.

Starting from the outer edge of a 14-inch oval gratin dish, arrange the shrimp in a single layer cut side down with the tails curling up and toward the center of the dish. Pour the remaining marinade over the shrimp. Spread the butter mixture evenly over the shrimp. Bake for 10 to 12 minutes, until hot and bubbly. If you like the top browned, place under a broiler for 1 minute. Serve with lemon wedges.

easy sole meunière

serves 2

One day in Paris, I decided to challenge myself and just go to the market with no menu in mind. Dover sole was in season and I thought, "Well, I can make sole meunière without a recipe, can't I?" Yes, I could! I was shocked by how easy and delicious it was. Of course, Dover sole is the best, but you can certainly use gray sole fillets from any fish store. The slightly burnt butter and the fresh lemon zest give this dish a big fresh lemon flavor. I serve two fillets per person.

- 1/2 **cup all-purpose flour**
- **Kosher salt and freshly ground black pepper**
- 4 **fresh sole fillets, 3 to 4 ounces each**
- 6 **tablespoons unsalted butter**
- 1 **teaspoon grated lemon zest**
- 6 **tablespoons freshly squeezed lemon juice (3 lemons)**
- 1 **tablespoon minced fresh parsley**

Preheat the oven to 200 degrees. Have 2 heat-proof dinner plates ready.

Combine the flour, 2 teaspoons salt, and 1 teaspoon pepper in a large shallow plate. Pat the sole fillets dry with paper towels and sprinkle one side with salt.

Heat 3 tablespoons of the butter in a large (12-inch) sauté pan over medium heat until it starts to brown. Dredge 2 sole fillets in the seasoned flour on both sides and place them in the hot butter. Lower the heat to medium-low and cook for 2 minutes. Turn carefully with a metal spatula and cook for 2 minutes on the other side. While the second side cooks, add 1/2 teaspoon of the lemon zest and 3 tablespoons of the lemon juice to the pan. Carefully put the fish fillets on the ovenproof plates and pour the sauce over them. Keep the cooked fillets warm in the oven while you repeat the process with the remaining 2 fillets. When they're done, add the cooked fillets to the plates in the oven. Sprinkle with the parsley, salt, and pepper and serve immediately.

Zest the lemons with a rasp before you squeeze them for their juice. This dish cooks quickly so I prepare all the ingredients before I start cooking.

bay scallop gratins

makes 3 gratins

Bay scallops are smaller, sweeter, and more tender than sea scallops and are generally only available on the East Coast. They're in season during the fall months. If you can't find them, sea scallops cut in quarters are also delicious and are available from the fall to the spring. Scallops can be pretty boring but the prosciutto, Pernod, and white wine give this dish lots of flavor. A squeeze of fresh lemon juice gives it the perfect finish.

    3 tablespoons unsalted butter, at room temperature
    3 large garlic cloves, minced
    1 medium shallot, minced
    1 ounce thinly sliced prosciutto di Parma, minced
    2 tablespoons minced fresh parsley, plus extra for garnish
    1 tablespoon freshly squeezed lemon juice
    1 tablespoon Pernod
    1 teaspoon kosher salt
    $1/2$ teaspoon freshly ground black pepper
    3 tablespoons good olive oil
    $1/4$ cup panko (Japanese dried bread flakes)
    3 tablespoons dry white wine
    1 pound fresh bay scallops
    Lemon, for garnish

Preheat the oven to 425 degrees. Place 3 (6-inch round) gratin dishes on a sheet pan.

To make the topping, place the butter in the bowl of an electric mixer fitted with the paddle attachment (you can also use a hand mixer). With the mixer on low speed, add the garlic, shallot, prosciutto, parsley, lemon juice, Pernod, salt, and pepper and mix until combined. With the mixer still on low, add the olive oil slowly as though making mayonnaise, until combined. Fold the panko in with a rubber spatula and set aside.

Preheat the broiler, if it's separate from your oven.

Place 1 tablespoon of the wine in the bottom of each gratin dish. With a small sharp knife, remove the white muscle and membrane from the side of each scallop and discard. Pat the scallops dry with paper towels and distribute them among the 3 dishes. Spoon the garlic butter evenly over the top of the scallops. Bake for 10 to 12 minutes, until the topping is golden and sizzling and the scallops are barely done. If you want the top crustier, place the dishes under the broiler for 2 minutes, until browned. Finish with a squeeze of fresh lemon juice and a sprinkling of chopped parsley and serve immediately with crusty French bread.

indonesian grilled swordfish

serves 6

Jeffrey loves my Indonesian ginger chicken so I came up with a grilling marinade for swordfish with the same soy sauce, lemon zest, ginger, and garlic flavors. Soy sauce acts as a tenderizer so it's terrific to marinate this overnight, but don't leave it any longer or the swordfish will become mushy.

1/3 cup soy sauce

1/4 cup canola or peanut oil, plus extra for brushing the grill

2 teaspoons grated lemon zest (2 lemons)

1/4 cup freshly squeezed lemon juice

1/4 cup minced or finely chopped fresh ginger (see note)

2 tablespoons minced garlic (4 cloves)

2 tablespoons Dijon mustard

6 (8-ounce, 1-inch-thick) swordfish steaks

Kosher salt

I use Kikkoman soy sauce.

Peel the ginger first and then mince it with a knife or chop it finely in a mini food processor.

Combine the soy sauce, canola oil, lemon zest, lemon juice, ginger, garlic, and mustard in a bowl. Pour half the sauce in a low flat dish that's just large enough to hold the swordfish in one layer. Place the swordfish on top of the sauce and spread the remaining sauce on top. Cover with plastic wrap and refrigerate for at least 4 hours or preferably overnight.

Thirty minutes before you're ready to serve, build a charcoal fire or heat a gas grill.

When the coals are medium-hot, brush the cooking grate with oil to prevent the fish from sticking. Remove the fish from the marinade, allowing some of the ginger to cling to the fish, and discard the marinade. Sprinkle the fish generously on both sides with salt and place it over the coals. Cook for 5 minutes on each side, just until it's no longer pink in the middle. Place on a platter, cover tightly with aluminum foil, and allow to rest for 10 to 15 minutes. Serve hot or warm.

mustard-roasted fish

serves 4

Nothing's easier than this roasted fish! It only takes ten minutes to make and it's good enough to serve to the fanciest company. This recipe comes from my Parisian friend Myriam Richard-Delorme, who's a wonderful cook. She serves it simply with steamed new potatoes and sautéed French haricots verts. How chic is that?

4 (8-ounce) fish fillets such as red snapper
Kosher salt and freshly ground black pepper
8 ounces crème fraîche
3 tablespoons Dijon mustard
1 tablespoon whole-grain mustard
2 tablespoons minced shallots
2 teaspoons drained capers

Preheat the oven to 425 degrees.

Line a sheet pan with parchment paper. (You can also use an ovenproof baking dish.) Place the fish fillets skin side down on the sheet pan. Sprinkle generously with salt and pepper.

Combine the crème fraîche, two mustards, shallots, capers, 1 teaspoon salt, and ½ teaspoon pepper in a small bowl. Spoon the sauce evenly over the fish fillets, making sure the fish is completely covered. Bake for 10 to 15 minutes, depending on the thickness of the fish, until it's barely done. (The fish will flake easily at the thickest part when it's done.) Be sure not to overcook it! Serve hot or at room temperature with the sauce from the pan spooned over the top.

soft-shell crab sandwiches

serves 6

I love crabmeat, but it's so much trouble to get out of the shell. From spring to early autumn, blue crabs shed their hard shells a few times and you can buy them in what's called the "soft" shell and eat them whole, shell and all. Ask the fishmonger to clean the live crabs for you because it's not a pretty task; but you'll need to cook them right away once they've been cleaned. This is a classic sandwich with a really flavorful cold rémoulade to contrast with the hot crabmeat.

FOR THE RÉMOULADE

1 cup good mayonnaise

¼ cup cornichons, drained and diced (5 cornichons)

3 tablespoons minced fresh dill

1 tablespoon capers, drained

2 teaspoons Dijon mustard

1 teaspoon anchovy paste

1 teaspoon grated lemon zest

1 tablespoon freshly squeezed lemon juice

½ teaspoon freshly ground black pepper

FOR THE CRABS

6 fresh soft-shell crabs, cleaned

1 cup whole milk

½ cup buttermilk, shaken

1 cup all-purpose flour

½ cup pecans

1 teaspoon kosher salt

½ teaspoon freshly ground black pepper

½ teaspoon cayenne pepper

3 tablespoons vegetable oil

2 tablespoons unsalted butter

FOR SERVING

6 fresh kaiser rolls, split

Boston lettuce leaves

12 slices beefsteak tomatoes (2 to 3 tomatoes)

For the rémoulade, combine the mayonnaise, cornichons, dill, capers, mustard, anchovy paste, lemon zest, lemon juice, and pepper in a small bowl. Cover and refrigerate until ready to use.

To prepare the soft-shell crabs, place the cleaned crabs in a single layer in a shallow dish and pour the milk and buttermilk over them. Let the crabs soak in the milk mixture at room temperature, flipping them over once, for 10 to 15 minutes.

Meanwhile, put the flour, pecans, salt, pepper, and cayenne in a food processor and process until the pecans are finely chopped and everything is evenly combined. Transfer the mixture to a wide, shallow dish, such as a pie plate. Remove the crabs from their milk bath and dredge them in the flour mixture, shaking off the excess.

Heat the oil and butter together in a very large, heavy skillet over medium-high heat. Sauté the crabs, top side down, until nicely browned, 2 to 3 minutes. To make the crabs extra crispy, weigh them down with a bacon or panini press or other heavy object such as a cast-iron skillet. Flip the crabs over and continue sautéing and pressing them down until the undersides are golden, 2 to 3 minutes more.

To assemble the sandwiches, spread both the top and bottom halves of the kaiser rolls generously with the rémoulade. Place a lettuce leaf and 2 tomato slices on the bottom halves of each roll. Top with a hot soft-shell crab, another lettuce leaf, and the top halves of the rolls. Serve at once with plenty of napkins, and eat by squishing the sandwich gently together so that the fresh bread absorbs the rémoulade sauce and some of the juices from the soft-shell crabs.

prosciutto roasted bass with autumn vegetables

serves 6

I tend to stay away from "restaurant-style" dishes because they take too much time to make at home. At the end of one of my book tours, I treated my wonderful assistant, Barbara, to dinner at Spago in Beverly Hills. Every meal I've ever had at Spago has knocked me out, but this dish I loved so much I decided to try something similar at home. It takes a little extra effort to cut and chop the vegetables but you can assemble it all in advance and bake it before dinner. I love the contrasts of the sweet vegetables, the tender fish, and the salty prosciutto.

This dish can also be made with other fish, such as salmon or sea bass, but the cooking time varies with the thickness of the fish. Cook the fish until it just flakes in the center.

2 cups peeled, seeded, and (½-inch) diced butternut squash

2 cups peeled and (½-inch) diced Yukon Gold potatoes (2 medium)

2 cups peeled and (½-inch) diced parsnips (3 parsnips)

2 cups peeled and (½-inch) diced carrots (6 carrots)

Good olive oil

Kosher salt and freshly ground black pepper

1 tablespoon minced garlic (3 cloves)

6 (8-ounce) skinless fish fillets such as striped bass or halibut

6 thin slices prosciutto di Parma

¼ pound (1 stick) unsalted butter

6 sprigs fresh rosemary

3 tablespoons freshly squeezed lemon juice

Lemon wedges, for serving

Preheat the oven to 400 degrees.

For the vegetables, place the butternut squash, potatoes, parsnips, and carrots on a sheet pan and drizzle with ⅓ cup olive oil. Sprinkle with 1 tablespoon salt and 1 teaspoon pepper and toss together. Spread out in a single layer and roast for 30 minutes, turning once during cooking. After 30 minutes, toss with the garlic and roast for another 10 minutes, until all the vegetables are tender and starting to brown.

(recipe continues)

Meanwhile, line another sheet pan with aluminum foil, and place a baking rack on top of the foil. Brush the fish fillets on both sides with olive oil and season them liberally with salt and pepper. Wrap each fillet with a slice of prosciutto to form a wide band around the center of the fillet, overlapping the ends on the skin side. Arrange the fillets on the rack with the prosciutto seam side down and roast for 10 to 15 minutes, until barely cooked.

While the vegetables and fish are roasting, melt the butter over medium heat in a medium-size sauté pan. Add the rosemary sprigs and cook over low heat until the rosemary leaves are crisp and the butter begins to brown, about 5 minutes. Discard the rosemary, stir in the lemon juice, and set aside.

To serve, place the fish on a platter or individual plates, spoon the rosemary butter on top, and surround with the vegetables. Garnish with lemon wedges and serve hot.

A squeeze of lemon and a sprinkle of flaked sea salt before serving really bring out the flavor of the fish and the roasted vegetables.

pasta with pecorino & pepper

serves 2 for dinner, 3 for appetizer

Inspired by a famous Roman dish called cacio e pepe, *this is a good recipe to whip up for a quick dinner after you get home. I love the hot spicy peppercorns together with the deep flavor of good aged Pecorino.*

1 tablespoon whole black Tellicherry peppercorns
   Kosher salt
½ pound dried Italian egg pasta such as tagliarelle
1 cup freshly grated aged Pecorino cheese (4 ounces),
   plus extra for serving (see note)
2 tablespoons heavy cream
1 tablespoon unsalted butter
2 tablespoons minced fresh parsley

Grate the Pecorino on the smaller teardrop holes of a box grater.

Place the peppercorns in a mortar and pestle and crush them until you have a mixture of coarse and fine bits. (You can also grind them in a small food mill or coffee grinder.) Set aside.

Fill a large, heavy-bottomed pot with water and bring to a boil. Add 1 tablespoon salt and the pasta and cook according to the directions on the package until al dente. Ladle 1 cup of the pasta cooking water into a glass measuring cup and reserve it. Drain the pasta quickly in a colander and return the pasta to the pot with a lot of the pasta water still dripping.

Working quickly, with the heat on very low, toss the pasta with ½ cup of the grated Pecorino, the crushed peppercorns, cream, butter, parsley, and 1 teaspoon salt, tossing constantly. If the pasta seems dry, add some of the reserved cooking water. Off the heat, toss in the remaining ½ cup Pecorino. Serve immediately with a big bowl of extra grated Pecorino for sprinkling.

Aged Pecorino from Italy is a grating cheese and, like Parmesan, the longer it has aged, the sharper it tastes. It's important in this recipe to buy the best Pecorino you can find at a cheese shop.

wild mushroom risotto

serves 6

When she started working with me, my assistant, Barbara, thought she hated mushrooms because the only ones she knew were those white "button" mushrooms we used to buy at the grocery store. Once she discovered the world of porcini, morels, and shiitake mushrooms, she became a convert. This is a perfect quick autumn meal when it's cold outside, the mushrooms are plentiful, and you feel like a dinner that will warm your insides.

1 ounce dried morel mushrooms
½ pound fresh porcini or cremini mushrooms
4 cups chicken stock, preferably homemade (page 61)
6 tablespoons (¾ stick) unsalted butter
2 ounces pancetta, diced
½ cup chopped shallots (3 shallots)
1½ cups Arborio rice
½ cup dry white wine
½ teaspoon saffron threads
1 teaspoon kosher salt
½ teaspoon freshly ground black pepper
⅔ cup freshly grated Parmesan cheese, plus extra for serving

Place the dried morels in a bowl and pour 2 cups boiling water over them. Set aside for 30 minutes. Scoop the morels from the water with a slotted spoon, reserving the liquid. You should have 2 cups; if not, add water to make 2 cups. Drain the morels and rinse once more. If some of the mushrooms are large, cut into 2 or 3 pieces. Pour the mushroom liquid through a coffee filter or paper towel, discarding the gritty solids. Set the mushrooms and the liquid aside separately.

Meanwhile, remove and discard the stems of the porcini and rub any dirt off the caps with a damp paper towel. Don't rinse them! Slice thickly and set aside.

In a small saucepan, heat the chicken stock with the 2 cups of reserved mushroom liquid and bring to a simmer.

In a heavy-bottomed pot or Dutch oven, melt the butter and sauté the pancetta and shallots over medium-low heat for 5 minutes. Add the morels and porcini and sauté for another 5 minutes. Add the rice and stir to coat the grains with butter. Add the wine and cook for 2 minutes. Add 2 full ladles of the chicken stock mixture to the rice plus the saffron, salt, and pepper. Stir and simmer over low heat until the stock is absorbed, 5 to 10 minutes.

Continue to add the stock mixture, 2 ladles at a time, stirring every few minutes. Each time, cook until the mixture seems a little dry before adding more of the stock mixture. Continue until the rice is cooked through, but still al dente, about 25 to 30 minutes total. When done, the risotto should be thick and creamy and not at all dry. Off the heat, stir in the Parmesan cheese. Serve hot in bowls with extra cheese.

spring green risotto

serves 4 for dinner, 6 for appetizer

Risotto is a great last-minute dinner if you have most of the ingredients on hand. I think risottos taste best when you add seasonal ingredients such as asparagus and chives in spring or butternut squash and saffron in autumn. The creamy mascarpone in this recipe is balanced by the acidity of the fresh lemon juice. This is a very therapeutic dinner after a hectic day; I turn up the music, pour myself a nice glass of white wine, and stir away.

$1^1/_2$ tablespoons good olive oil

$1^1/_2$ tablespoons unsalted butter

3 cups chopped leeks, white and light green parts (2 leeks)

1 cup chopped fennel

$1^1/_2$ cups Arborio rice

$^2/_3$ cup dry white wine

4 to 5 cups simmering chicken stock, preferably homemade (page 61)

1 pound thin asparagus

10 ounces frozen peas, defrosted, or $1^1/_2$ cups shelled fresh peas

1 tablespoon freshly grated lemon zest (2 lemons)

Kosher salt and freshly ground black pepper

2 tablespoons freshly squeezed lemon juice

$^1/_3$ cup mascarpone cheese, preferably Italian

$^1/_2$ cup freshly grated Parmesan cheese, plus extra for serving

3 tablespoons minced fresh chives, plus extra for serving

Heat the olive oil and butter in a medium saucepan over medium heat. Add the leeks and fennel and sauté for 5 to 7 minutes, until tender. Add the rice and stir for a minute to coat with the vegetables, oil, and butter. Add the white wine and simmer over low heat, stirring constantly, until most of the wine has been absorbed. Add the chicken stock, 2 ladles at a time, stirring almost constantly and waiting for the stock to be absorbed before adding more. This process should take 25 to 30 minutes.

(recipe continues)

Meanwhile, cut the asparagus diagonally in 1¹/₂-inch lengths and discard the tough ends. Blanch in boiling salted water for 4 to 5 minutes, until al dente. Drain and cool immediately in ice water. (If using fresh peas, blanch them in boiling water for a few minutes until the starchiness is gone.)

When the risotto has been cooking for 15 minutes, drain the asparagus and add it to the risotto with the peas, lemon zest, 2 teaspoons salt, and 1 teaspoon pepper. Continue cooking and adding stock, stirring almost constantly, until the rice is tender but still firm.

Whisk the lemon juice and mascarpone together in a small bowl. When the risotto is done, turn off the heat and stir in the mascarpone mixture plus the Parmesan cheese and chives. Set aside off the heat for a few minutes, sprinkle with salt and pepper, and serve hot with a sprinkling of chives and more Parmesan cheese.

Mascarpone is an Italian cream cheese. You can find it in the grocery or at an Italian specialty store.

dinner spanakopitas

makes 12 strudels

Savory strudels are great for a cocktail party because you can make them, freeze them, and bake them before a party. At Barefoot Contessa, we also made them filled with curried crabmeat, or sausage, but spinach and feta strudels were always the most popular. They're usually made small to eat with cocktails, but I thought larger ones would be a great main course for a vegetarian dinner. My friends agreed.

¼ cup good olive oil
1 cup chopped yellow onion
3 scallions, white and green parts, chopped
2 (10-ounce) packages frozen chopped spinach, defrosted
4 extra-large eggs, lightly beaten
3 tablespoons freshly grated Parmesan cheese
Plain dry bread crumbs
1 teaspoon grated nutmeg
2 teaspoons kosher salt
1 teaspoon freshly ground black pepper
2 cups small-diced feta cheese (12 ounces)
3 tablespoons toasted pine nuts (page 43)
24 sheets frozen phyllo dough, defrosted
¼ pound (1 stick) unsalted butter, melted
Flaked sea salt, such as Maldon, for sprinkling

The phyllo dough I buy has two 8-ounce packages. Use one and keep one frozen for later.

The unbaked strudels can be wrapped and refrigerated or frozen and then baked before serving.

Preheat the oven to 375 degrees.

Heat the olive oil in a medium sauté pan, add the onion, and cook for 5 minutes over medium-low heat. Add the scallions, and cook for another 2 minutes until the scallions are wilted but still green. Meanwhile, gently squeeze most of the water out of the spinach and place it in a large bowl.

When the onion and scallions are done, add them to the

(recipe continues)

spinach. Mix in the eggs, Parmesan cheese, 3 tablespoons bread crumbs, the nutmeg, salt, and pepper. Gently fold in the feta and pine nuts.

Place one sheet of phyllo dough flat on a work surface with the long end in front of you. Brush the dough lightly with butter and sprinkle it with a teaspoon of bread crumbs. Working quickly, slide another sheet of phyllo dough on top of the first, brush it with butter, and sprinkle lightly with bread crumbs. (Use just enough bread crumbs so the layers of phyllo don't stick together.) Pile 4 layers total on top of each other this way, brushing each with butter and sprinkling with bread crumbs. Cut the sheets of phyllo in half lengthwise. Place $1/3$ cup spinach filling on the shorter end and roll the phyllo up diagonally as if folding a flag. Then fold the triangle of phyllo over straight and then diagonally again. Continue folding first diagonally and then straight until you reach the end of the sheet. The filling should be totally enclosed. Continue assembling phyllo layers and folding the filling until all of the filling is used. Place on a sheet pan, seam sides down. Brush with melted butter, sprinkle with flaked salt, and bake for 30 to 35 minutes, until the phyllo is browned and crisp. Serve hot.

tagliarelle with truffle butter

serves 2 or 3 for dinner, 4 or 5 for a side dish or appetizer

OMG is this delicious. I keep the key ingredients in my pantry and freezer so in fifteen minutes I can whip up a very fancy dinner. It's the essence of my philosophy: if you start with really good ingredients, you don't need to cook much to make something delicious. I buy Cipriani pasta at a specialty food store and three-ounce packages of white truffle butter from dartagnan.com and keep them on hand for a quick—but very special!—dinner.

White truffles are very expensive wild fungi from Italy's Piedmont region. I'm not a fan of white truffle oil (it sometimes has a metallic flavor), but D'Artagnan makes 3-ounce containers of truffle butter with pieces of white truffles. It's delicious and quite inexpensive.

Kosher salt

½ cup heavy cream

3 ounces white truffle butter (see note)

Freshly ground black pepper

1 (8.82-ounce) package Cipriani tagliarelle dried pasta or other egg fettuccine

3 tablespoons chopped fresh chives

3 ounces Parmesan, shaved thin with a vegetable peeler

Add 1 tablespoon salt to a large pot of water and bring to a boil.

Meanwhile, in a large (12-inch) sauté pan, heat the cream over medium heat until it comes to a simmer. Add the truffle butter, 1 teaspoon salt, and ½ teaspoon pepper, lower the heat to very low, and swirl the butter until it melts. Keep warm over very low heat.

Add the pasta to the boiling water and cook for 3 minutes, exactly. (If you're not using Cipriani pasta, follow the directions on the package.) When the pasta is cooked, reserve ½ cup of the cooking water, then drain the pasta. Add the drained pasta to the sauté pan and toss it with the truffle-cream mixture. As the pasta absorbs the sauce, add as much of the reserved cooking water as necessary to keep the pasta very creamy.

Serve the pasta in shallow bowls and garnish each serving with a generous sprinkling of chives and shaved Parmesan. Sprinkle with salt and pepper and serve at once.

vegetables

maple-roasted butternut squash

confetti corn

creamy cheddar grits

orange pecan wild rice

baked potatoes with yogurt

celery root & apple purée

oven-roasted vegetables

parmesan-roasted broccoli

chive risotto cakes

pan-roasted root vegetables

roasted parsnips & carrots

baked sweet potato "fries"

roasted tomatoes with basil

garlic ciabatta bread

set a table like a pro

1 For small groups, round tables are best: 48 inches for six people, 54 inches for eight. A 60-inch round is too large to talk across, so for ten or more I prefer a narrow rectangular table.

2 Make the flower arrangements at least a day in advance to allow the blooms to open fully.

3 Iron the tablecloth completely, removing any creases created when the cloth was folded. Store tablecloths rolled on cardboard tubes or hung on dowels to keep them pressed.

4 Iron napkins in flat squares. Fold and place them in the middle of the plate or to the left of the forks.

5 The knives and spoons go to the right of the plate and the forks go to the left. The utensils that are used first go to the outside (farthest from the plate). For example, the appetizer fork goes first, the main course fork goes to its right, and the dessert fork goes closest to the plate. The same is true for the knives, and the spoons are to the right of the knives. If you have a lot of utensils, the dessert spoon and fork can go at the top of the plate.

6 The glasses go to the top of the knife, the wineglass to the right of the water glass.

7 Place cards, if you're using them, go on the plate or on the table at the top of the plate.

8 Try to make the light on the table brighter than the ambient light in the room; it brings everyone's attention to the center and it makes a better party.

9 Choose low votive candles so your guests can see one another clearly.

10 Before you finish the setting, sit at the table to be sure you can see past the candles and flowers to the person who will sit on the other side.

maple-roasted butternut squash

serves 6

Butternut squash is one of my favorite vegetables and I usually roast it with a little butter and brown sugar. But I was looking for something more savory with just a touch of sweetness. The roasted garlic is amazing because it becomes tender and sweet when it's baked, and the pancetta gives the squash a nice salty bite. A sprinkling of coarse sea salt before serving really brings out the flavor.

1	large butternut squash
1	head garlic, separated but not peeled
2	tablespoons good olive oil
2½	tablespoons pure maple syrup
1	teaspoon kosher salt
½	teaspoon freshly ground black pepper
2	ounces thinly sliced pancetta, chopped
16	whole fresh sage leaves
	French bread, for serving

Preheat the oven to 400 degrees.

Peel and seed the butternut squash and then cut it into ¾- to 1-inch cubes. Place the squash and the whole unpeeled garlic cloves on a sheet pan in one layer. Toss with the olive oil, maple syrup, salt, and pepper and bake for 20 to 30 minutes, until the squash begins to brown, turning once during baking.

Sprinkle the pancetta and the sage leaves evenly over the butternut squash and continue to bake for another 20 to 30 minutes, until the squash and garlic are tender and caramelized. Season to taste and serve hot with French bread for guests to spread with the roasted garlic.

confetti corn

serves 6

When the corn is available at Jim Pike's farm stand, I have to rush right over and take some home. I usually just cut it off the cob and sauté it in butter with lots of salt and pepper, but I thought it would be fun to add more vegetables and herbs from the stand and the result was this colorful and flavorful dish that goes with anything from grilled hot dogs to grilled steak.

Cook corn as soon as possible after it's picked because the sugar turns to starch quickly.

2 tablespoons good olive oil

½ cup chopped red onion

1 small orange bell pepper, ½-inch diced

2 tablespoons unsalted butter

Kernels cut from 5 ears yellow or white corn (4 cups)

1½ teaspoons kosher salt

1 teaspoon freshly ground black pepper

2 tablespoons julienned fresh basil, minced fresh chives, and/or minced fresh parsley

Heat the olive oil over medium heat in a large sauté pan. Add the onion and sauté for 5 minutes, until the onion is soft. Stir in the bell pepper and sauté for 2 more minutes.

Add the butter to the pan and allow it to melt. Over medium heat, add the corn, salt, and pepper and cook, stirring occasionally, for 5 to 7 minutes, until the corn just loses its starchiness. Season to taste, gently stir in the basil or other green herbs, and serve hot.

creamy cheddar grits

serves 6

We all grew up on mashed potatoes, and then later I learned about polenta. But when I was introduced to grits, which—like polenta—is made from corn, I was hooked. It's such a delicious savory side dish, and this one with sharp Cheddar and scallions will surprise everyone. Be sure to use good aged Cheddar; it will make all the difference.

> 2 teaspoons kosher salt
> 1 cup fine quick-cooking grits (not instant)
> 1¼ cups half-and-half
> 2 tablespoons unsalted butter
> 1½ cups aged sharp Cheddar cheese, grated (4 ounces)
> ½ cup chopped scallions, white and green parts (4 scallions)
> ½ teaspoon freshly ground black pepper
> Grated Cheddar and chopped scallions, for garnish

Grits, or hominy grits, is made from dried white or yellow corn from which the hull and germ have been removed. It comes in fine, medium, and coarse grinds.

I use sharp, aged Grafton or Cabot Cheddar from Vermont.

Bring 4 cups of water to a boil in a heavy 4-quart saucepan. Add the salt, then slowly add the grits in a thin, steady stream, stirring constantly with a wooden spoon. Reduce the heat to low and simmer, stirring occasionally, until the grits thicken, about 5 to 7 minutes.

Add the half-and-half and butter to the grits and stir. The mixture will seem thin but it will thicken as it cooks. Bring to a simmer, stirring occasionally. Cover the pot, reduce the heat to low, and cook, stirring occasionally for 45 minutes, until very smooth and creamy. Off the heat, stir in the Cheddar, scallions, and pepper. Season to taste and serve hot with a sprinkle of grated cheese and scallions.

orange pecan wild rice

serves 6

We used to make wild rice salad at Barefoot Contessa, but I confess, I never really loved cold wild rice. However, we did make a warm wild rice for parties that I loved—with lots of butter and fresh pepper. I decided to combine the two recipes and make a hot wild rice dish with grapes, scallions, and orange zest. And voilà! It's the best of both recipes!

1 cup wild rice

1¼ cups chicken stock, preferably homemade (page 61)

2 tablespoons unsalted butter

Kosher salt

1 cup seedless green grapes, halved

½ cup scallions, sliced in rounds, white and light green parts (2 scallions)

1 cup pecan halves, toasted (see note) and coarsely chopped

1 teaspoon grated orange zest

2 tablespoons freshly squeezed orange juice

1 teaspoon freshly ground black pepper

Spread the pecans on a sheet pan and toast in a 350-degree oven for 8 minutes. Let the pecans cool completely before chopping.

Place the rice, chicken stock, 1¼ cups water, 1 tablespoon of the butter, and 1 teaspoon salt in a medium saucepan and bring to a boil over medium heat. Cover the pot and lower the heat to simmer (I pull the pan halfway off the burner) and cook for about 1 hour, until the rice is tender and the grains begin to burst open. Stir the rice occasionally while it's cooking, scraping the bottom of the pan to prevent it from sticking. Turn off the heat and allow the rice to steam for about 5 minutes.

Stir the remaining tablespoon of butter into the rice, then add the grapes, scallions, pecans, orange zest, orange juice, 1 teaspoon salt, and the pepper and toss well. Taste for seasonings and serve hot.

baked potatoes with yogurt & sour cream

serves 4

Who doesn't love baked potatoes with sour cream? I wanted the old-fashioned flavor but I also wanted to make them lighter and a little more special . . . so I whipped up a yogurt and sour cream dressing with lots of fresh chives. Of course, these potatoes are delicious with grilled steaks or roast chicken.

I use the Fage Total brand of Greek yogurt.

4 **Idaho russet baking potatoes**

1/2 **cup Greek yogurt**

1/2 **cup sour cream**

2 **tablespoons chopped fresh chives, plus extra for garnish**
   Kosher salt and freshly ground black pepper

Preheat the oven to 350 degrees.

Wash the potatoes and place them directly on the oven baking rack. Bake for 45 to 60 minutes, until very tender when pierced with a skewer.

Meanwhile, combine the yogurt, sour cream, chives, 1/2 teaspoon salt, and 1/4 teaspoon pepper and place in a serving bowl. Garnish with extra chives. Chill.

When the potatoes are done, cut them down the middle and squeeze both ends. Sprinkle with salt and pepper and serve the hot baked potatoes with the cold chive dressing.

celery root & apple purée

serves 4 to 6

In winter when all the leafy green vegetables are flown in from Chile, I prefer to make purées of local winter vegetables. This is such a delicious (and easy!) vegetable purée to make and it's the perfect thing to serve with a pork roast or chicken. Of course, you can purée this in a food processor, but it has so much more texture if it's processed through a food mill instead. It's thick and full of the flavors of fennel, celery root, potato, and apple. I finish it with sea salt before serving.

$^{1}/_{4}$ **pound (1 stick) unsalted butter**

1 **cup large-diced fennel bulb, tops and core removed**

2 **pounds celery root, peeled and $^{3}/_{4}$-inch diced**

8 **ounces Yukon Gold potatoes, peeled and $^{3}/_{4}$-inch diced**

3 **Golden Delicious apples, peeled, cored, and $^{3}/_{4}$-inch diced**

Kosher salt and freshly ground black pepper

$^{1}/_{2}$ **cup good apple cider**

$^{1}/_{4}$ **cup heavy cream**

The trick to cutting a hard root vegetable, such as this celery root, without a trip to the hospital is to peel it and cut it in half. Place the flat cut side on the board and then dice the vegetable.

To make in advance, refrigerate for up to 4 days and reheat slowly with a little added apple cider or cream.

Melt the butter over medium heat in a shallow stock pot or large sauté pan. Add the fennel, celery root, potatoes, apples, 1$^{1}/_{2}$ teaspoons salt, and $^{1}/_{2}$ teaspoon pepper. Sauté the vegetables, stirring occasionally, until they begin to soften, about 4 to 5 minutes. Add the cider and tightly cover the pot. Simmer over low heat (I pull the pot halfway off the heat) for 30 to 40 minutes, stirring occasionally, until the vegetables are very soft. If the vegetables begin to burn or they seem dry, add another few tablespoons of apple cider or some water.

When the vegetables are cooked, add the cream and cook for 1 more minute. Transfer the mixture to a food mill fitted with the coarsest blade and process. (You can also use a food processor but the texture will be smoother than with the food mill.) Taste for salt and pepper and return to the pot to keep warm. Serve warm.

oven-roasted vegetables

serves 6

There's a recipe for roasted fennel and potatoes that I've always loved in The New Basics Cookbook *by Julee Rosso and Sheila Lukins of the Silver Palate. I decided to do my own variation on it with asparagus and Parmesan cheese. All the vegetables are roasted together on one sheet pan and it's everything you need to serve with a nice roast chicken or veal chop. A hit of Parmesan cheese at the end gives all the vegetables great flavor.*

    2 small fennel bulbs, tops removed

    1 pound fingerling or small potatoes

    1/3 cup good olive oil

       Kosher salt and freshly ground black pepper

    1 pound French string beans (haricots verts), trimmed

    1 bunch thin asparagus, ends removed, cut diagonally
       into 3-inch pieces

    1/4 cup freshly grated Parmesan cheese

Preheat the oven to 425 degrees.

Cut the fennel bulbs into 6 wedges each, cutting through the core to keep the wedges intact. Place on a sheet pan. Cut the potatoes in half lengthwise and place them on the pan with the fennel. Drizzle the olive oil on the vegetables, then sprinkle with 2 teaspoons salt and 1 teaspoon pepper. Toss with your hands.

Roast the vegetables for 25 to 30 minutes, until the potatoes are tender, tossing once while cooking. Toss the string beans and asparagus with the roasted vegetables and roast for another 10 to 15 minutes, until the green vegetables are tender. Sprinkle on the Parmesan cheese and roast for another minute or two until the cheese melts.

Sprinkle with salt and pepper and serve hot.

parmesan-roasted broccoli

serves 6

Broccoli is one of the green vegetables that's available year-round. Look for firm heads with tight florets and stalks with green leaves. I cut the broccoli in florets with about an inch or two of stem below the head but you can peel the stems and use them, too, if you prefer. Roasting the broccoli with garlic and Parmesan gives this dish great flavor.

4 to 5 pounds broccoli
4 garlic cloves, peeled and thinly sliced
Good olive oil
$1^{1}/_2$ teaspoons kosher salt
$^{1}/_2$ teaspoon freshly ground black pepper
2 teaspoons grated lemon zest
2 tablespoons freshly squeezed lemon juice
3 tablespoons pine nuts, toasted (page 43)
$^{1}/_3$ cup freshly grated Parmesan cheese
2 tablespoons julienned fresh basil leaves (about 12 leaves)

Preheat the oven to 425 degrees.

Cut the broccoli florets from the thick stalks, leaving an inch or two of stalk attached to the florets, discarding the rest of the stalks. Cut the larger pieces through the base of the head with a small knife, pulling the florets apart. You should have about 8 cups of florets. Place the broccoli florets on a sheet pan large enough to hold them in a single layer. Toss the garlic on the broccoli and drizzle with 5 tablespoons olive oil. Sprinkle with the salt and pepper. Roast for 20 to 25 minutes, until crisp-tender and the tips of some of the florets are browned.

Remove the broccoli from the oven and immediately toss with $1^{1}/_2$ tablespoons olive oil, the lemon zest, lemon juice, pine nuts, Parmesan, and basil. Serve hot.

chive risotto cakes

serves 6

I used to have to wait until I made risotto in order to make risotto cakes from the leftovers. So I decided to do a recipe for risotto cakes that I make from scratch. Most of this can be assembled early in the day and then sautéed just before dinner. The yogurt, chives, and Italian Fontina give these a delicious creamy interior, and the panko gives them a wonderful crunchy crust.

Panko, or Japanese bread flakes, have a crisper, lighter texture than regular bread crumbs.

Kosher salt
1 cup uncooked Arborio rice
1/2 cup Greek yogurt
2 extra-large eggs
3 tablespoons minced fresh chives
1 1/2 cups grated Italian Fontina cheese (5 ounces)
1/2 teaspoon freshly ground black pepper
3/4 cup panko (Japanese dried bread flakes)
Good olive oil

Bring a large (4-quart) pot of water to a boil and add 1/2 tablespoon salt and the Arborio rice. Cook, stirring occasionally, for 20 minutes. The grains of rice will be quite soft. Drain the rice in a sieve and run under cold water until cool. Drain well.

Meanwhile, whisk together the yogurt, eggs, chives, Fontina, 1 1/4 teaspoons salt, and the pepper in a medium bowl. Add the cooled rice and mix well. Cover with plastic wrap and refrigerate for 2 hours or overnight, until firm.

When ready to cook, preheat the oven to 250 degrees.

Spread the panko in a shallow dish. Heat 3 tablespoons olive oil in a large skillet over medium-low heat. Form balls of the rice mixture using a standard (2 1/4-inch) ice-cream scoop or a large spoon. Pat the balls into patties 3 inches in diameter and 3/4 inch thick. Place 4 to 6 patties in the panko, turning once to coat. Place the patties in the hot oil and cook, turning once, for about 3 minutes on each side until the risotto cakes are crisp and nicely browned. Place on a sheet pan lined with parchment paper and keep warm in the oven for up to 30 minutes. Continue cooking in batches, adding oil as necessary, until all the cakes are fried. Serve hot.

pan-roasted root vegetables

serves 4

My friend Anna Pump and I went to one of my favorite restaurants together—Blue Hill at Stone Barns—and were served a mélange of root vegetables cooked in a little butter on top of the stove. The vegetables got a little browned but they basically steamed in their own juices. Of course, Stone Barns grows their own gorgeous organic baby vegetables, but I was happy to discover that I could get some of the same wonderful flavors with vegetables from the store. This dish is surprisingly simple to make yet so delicious.

If you want to double this recipe, make it in two batches or use two (12-inch) sauté pans. You want the vegetables to brown on the bottom as well as steam in their own juices.

4 tablespoons (½ stick) unsalted butter
1 white turnip, unpeeled and 1-inch diced
2 carrots, 1-inch diced (preferably from carrots with the greens attached)
2 small parsnips, peeled and 1-inch diced
½ celery root, peeled and 1-inch diced
8 Brussels sprouts, halved if large
4 fresh thyme sprigs
1½ teaspoons kosher salt
½ teaspoon freshly ground black pepper
2 celery ribs, 1-inch diced

Melt the butter in a large (12-inch) sauté pan that has a tight-fitting lid. When the butter is melted, add the turnip, carrots, parsnips, celery root, Brussels sprouts, thyme, salt, and pepper and toss with the butter. Cover the pan and cook over low heat for 10 minutes. Add the celery and stir the vegetables. Cover the pan again and continue to cook for another 5 minutes, until all the vegetables are tender. If they're too dry, add a few tablespoons of water. Taste for seasonings and serve hot.

roasted parsnips & carrots

serves 4

Everyone knows carrots, but parsnips are really an underappreciated vegetable. They're white, they look like carrots, and they're sweet like carrots. When you see them in the grocery store, you'll wonder why you never cooked them before. Choose small parsnips, because the large ones tend to have woody cores. Sometimes they have tough outsides so I peel them, while carrots are more tender so I just scrub them with a vegetable brush.

> 2 pounds parsnips, peeled
> 1 pound carrots, unpeeled
> 3 tablespoons good olive oil
> 1 tablespoon kosher salt
> 1½ teaspoons freshly ground black pepper
> 2 tablespoons minced fresh dill or parsley

Preheat the oven to 425 degrees.

If the parsnips and carrots are very thick, cut them in half lengthwise. Slice each one diagonally in 1-inch-thick slices. The vegetables will shrink while cooking, so don't make the pieces too small. Place the cut vegetables on a sheet pan. Add the olive oil, salt, and pepper and toss well. Roast for 20 to 40 minutes, depending on the size of the vegetables, tossing occasionally, until the parsnips and carrots are just tender. Sprinkle with dill and serve hot.

Choose topped carrots (with their greens attached) and parsnips that are white and firm to the touch.

baked sweet potato "fries"

serves 4

Sweet potatoes are available year-round, but their prime season is really autumn and winter. Choose potatoes that are smooth and unblemished, and use them fairly soon because they don't keep as well as other potatoes. These potatoes are crispy like fries but they're better for you because they're baked.

2 medium sweet potatoes, peeled
2 tablespoons good olive oil
1 tablespoon light brown sugar
$^1/_2$ teaspoon kosher salt, plus extra for sprinkling
$^1/_2$ teaspoon freshly ground black pepper

Preheat the oven to 450 degrees.

Halve the sweet potatoes lengthwise and cut each half into 3 long spears. Place them on a sheet pan and toss with the olive oil. Spread the potatoes in one layer. Combine the brown sugar, salt, and pepper and sprinkle on the potatoes. Bake for 15 minutes and then turn with a spatula. Bake for another 5 to 10 minutes, until lightly browned. Sprinkle lightly with salt and serve hot.

roasted tomatoes with basil

serves 4 to 5

It's a challenge to take something pedestrian from the grocery store and make it really delicious. Plum tomatoes are available year-round but they generally have absolutely no flavor. I discovered that if I roast them at a high temperature with good balsamic vinegar, they develop the intense flavor of summer tomatoes. I serve these with roast chicken, turkey meatloaf (The Barefoot Contessa Cookbook), or grilled steaks.

12 plum tomatoes, halved lengthwise, seeds (not cores) removed
1/4 cup good olive oil
1 1/2 tablespoons aged balsamic vinegar
2 large garlic cloves, minced
2 teaspoons sugar
1 1/2 teaspoons kosher salt
1/2 teaspoon freshly ground black pepper
10 large fresh basil leaves, julienned

Preheat the oven to 450 degrees.

Arrange the tomatoes on a sheet pan, cut sides up, in a single layer. Drizzle with the olive oil and balsamic vinegar. Sprinkle with the garlic, sugar, salt, and pepper. Roast for 25 to 30 minutes, until the tomatoes start to caramelize and the flavors are concentrated. Sprinkle the basil on top and serve warm or at room temperature.

garlic ciabatta bread

serves 6

This is old-fashioned garlic bread but made with good ingredients: lots of chopped fresh garlic and herbs slathered on ciabatta bread. The whole house smells good when you make this.

6 large garlic cloves, chopped
1/4 cup fresh parsley
2 tablespoons fresh oregano leaves
1 teaspoon kosher salt
1/2 teaspoon freshly ground black pepper
1/2 cup good olive oil
1 large ciabatta bread
2 tablespoons unsalted butter, at room temperature

Preheat the oven to 350 degrees.

Place the garlic, parsley, oregano, salt, and pepper in the bowl of a food processor fitted with the steel blade and process until finely minced. Heat the olive oil in a medium sauté pan over low heat. Add the garlic and herb mixture and cook for 3 minutes, until the garlic is tender but not browned. Remove from the heat and set aside.

Cut the ciabatta in half horizontally, running a serrated knife parallel to the board. Spoon the garlic mixture onto the bottom half and spread the butter on the top half and place together. Wrap the bread in aluminum foil and place on a sheet pan.

Bake the bread for 5 minutes, then unwrap and discard the foil. Bake for another 5 minutes. Slice crosswise and serve warm.

dessert

french apple tart

fresh lemon mousse

apple dried cherry turnovers

chocolate-dipped strawberries

french chocolate bark

old-fashioned gingerbread

plum crunch

honey vanilla fromage blanc

honey vanilla pound cake

fresh raspberry gratins

pumpkin roulade

raisin pecan oatmeal cookies

affogato sundaes

brownie pudding

10 *no-cook* things to serve for dessert

1 Vanilla ice cream drizzled with saba

2 Fresh pears, English Stilton, and aged port wine

3 Vanilla ice cream mixed with chopped crystallized ginger and store-bought almond biscotti

4 Store-bought brownies, coffee ice cream, and chocolate sauce

5 Store-bought pound cake toasted and drizzled with honey and fresh raspberries

6 Clementines, dates, good chocolates, and demi-sec champagne

7 Passionfruit sorbet and vanilla ice cream with Grey Goose vodka poured on top

8 Strawberries macerated with sugar and good balsamic vinegar

9 Store-bought chocolate cake with melted vanilla Häagen-Dazs ice cream as a sauce and fresh raspberries

10 Macoun apples, English Cheddar, and store-bought ginger cookies

french apple tart

serves 6

This just might be my all-time favorite dessert. It's the simple essence of sweet apples and crisp pastry with no distractions. We've all collected several similar recipes over the years, but this is the best one I've ever made. If I need to make it even faster, I use defrosted frozen puff pastry instead of making the crust (see note), but you'll want to eat it an hour or two after it comes out of the oven.

FOR THE PASTRY

> 2 cups all-purpose flour
>
> ¹/₂ teaspoon kosher salt
>
> 1 tablespoon sugar
>
> 12 tablespoons (1¹/₂ sticks) cold unsalted butter, diced
>
> ¹/₂ cup ice water

FOR THE APPLES

> 4 Granny Smith apples
>
> ¹/₂ cup sugar
>
> 4 tablespoons (¹/₂ stick) cold unsalted butter, small-diced
>
> ¹/₂ cup apricot jelly or warm sieved apricot jam (see note)
>
> 2 tablespoons Calvados, rum, or water

For a really fast apple tart, you can use one sheet of frozen puff pastry, defrosted. Roll out to 10¹/₂ × 10¹/₂ inches and then proceed with the apples.

For the pastry, place the flour, salt, and sugar in the bowl of a food processor fitted with the steel blade. Pulse for a few seconds to combine. Add the butter and pulse 10 to 12 times, until the butter is in small bits the size of peas. With the motor running, pour the ice water down the feed tube and pulse just until the dough starts to come together. Dump onto a floured board and knead quickly into a ball. Wrap in plastic and refrigerate for at least 1 hour.

Preheat the oven to 400 degrees. Line a sheet pan with parchment paper.

(recipe continues)

Roll the dough slightly larger than 10 × 14 inches. Using a ruler and a small knife, trim the edges. Place the dough on the prepared sheet pan and refrigerate while you prepare the apples.

If you can only find apricot jam, heat it first and then sieve it before making the glaze.

Peel the apples and cut them in half through the stem. Remove the stems and cores with a sharp knife and a melon baller. Slice the apples crosswise in 1/4-inch-thick slices. Place overlapping slices of apples diagonally down the middle of the tart and continue making diagonal rows on both sides of the first row until the pastry is covered with apple slices. (I tend not to use the apple ends in order to make the arrangement beautiful.) Sprinkle with the full 1/2 cup sugar and dot with the butter.

Bake for 45 minutes to 1 hour, until the pastry is browned and the edges of the apples start to brown. Rotate the pan once during cooking. If the pastry puffs up in one area, cut a little slit with a knife to let the air out. Don't worry! The apple juices will burn in the pan but the tart will be fine! When the tart's done, heat the apricot jelly together with the Calvados and brush the apples *and* the pastry completely with the jelly mixture. Loosen the tart with a metal spatula so it doesn't stick to the paper. Allow to cool and serve warm or at room temperature.

fresh lemon mousse

serves 6

Freshly squeezed lemon juice is an essential element of my cooking. I almost always add the grated lemon zest because there's even more flavor in the zest than in the juice. This is easy to make in advance and delicious on a hot summer night.

3 extra-large whole eggs
3 extra-large eggs, separated
1 cup plus 2 tablespoons sugar
2 teaspoons grated lemon zest
1/2 cup freshly squeezed lemon juice (4 lemons)
   Kosher salt
1 cup heavy cream
1/2 cup good bottled lemon curd, at room temperature
   Sweetened Whipped Cream (recipe follows)
   Sliced lemon, for garnish

Room-temperature lemons give more juice. Roll them on a board to release the juices before squeezing.

In a large heat-proof bowl, whisk together the 3 whole eggs, 3 egg yolks, 1 cup sugar, the lemon zest, lemon juice, and a pinch of salt. Place the bowl over a pan of simmering water and cook, stirring constantly with a wooden spoon, for about 10 to 12 minutes, until the mixture is thick like pudding. (I change to a whisk when the mixture starts to get thick.) Take off the heat and set aside for 15 minutes. Cover with plastic wrap directly on the surface and refrigerate for 1 to 2 hours, until completely chilled.

Place half the egg whites and a pinch of salt in the bowl of an electric mixer fitted with the whisk attachment. Beat on high speed. Add the remaining 2 tablespoons sugar and continue to beat until the whites are stiff and shiny. Carefully fold the beaten whites into the cold lemon mixture with a rubber spatula. Place the cream in the same bowl of the electric mixer fitted with the whisk attachment (no need to clean the bowl) and beat on high speed until the cream forms stiff peaks. Carefully fold the whipped cream into the lemon mixture. Fold in the lemon curd and pour into a 7-inch-diameter, 3-inch-deep soufflé dish. Decorate with sweetened whipped cream and lemon slices that have been cut into quarters. Chill and serve cold.

sweetened whipped cream

    1 cup cold heavy cream
    1 tablespoon sugar
1/2 teaspoon pure vanilla extract

Place the cream, sugar, and vanilla in the bowl of an electric mixer fitted with the whisk attachment. Whip on medium and then high speed until the cream just forms stiff peaks. Spoon the whipped cream into a pastry bag fitted with a large star tip.

My soufflé dish measures 7 inches in diameter on the top and 6 1/4 inches in diameter on the bottom.

apple dried cherry turnovers

makes 8

Sometimes one or two ingredients are just the thing to give a favorite recipe a twist. I wanted to make apple turnovers but instead of making piecrust for the dough, I used frozen puff pastry from the grocery store. They turned out not only easier to make but also so much more elegant! The apple filling is a little sweet, with classic apple-pie spices and dried cherries.

Defrost puff pastry overnight in the refrigerator.

Choose tart apples that are crisp, such as Macoun, Granny Smith, or Winesaps.

1 teaspoon grated orange zest
3 tablespoons freshly squeezed orange juice
1¼ pounds tart apples (3 apples)
3 tablespoons dried cherries
3 tablespoons sugar, plus extra for sprinkling
1 tablespoon all-purpose flour
¼ teaspoon ground cinnamon
⅛ teaspoon ground nutmeg
    Pinch of kosher salt
1 package (17.3 ounces/2 sheets) frozen puff pastry, defrosted
1 egg beaten with 1 tablespoon water, for egg wash

Preheat the oven to 400 degrees.

Combine the orange zest and orange juice in a medium bowl. Peel, quarter, and core the apples and then cut them into ¾-inch dice. Immediately toss the apples with the zest and juice to prevent them from turning brown. Add the cherries, sugar, flour, cinnamon, nutmeg, and salt.

Flour a board and lightly roll each sheet of puff pastry to a 12 × 12-inch square. Cut each sheet into 4 (6 × 6-inch) squares and keep chilled until ready to use.

Brush the edges of each square with the egg wash and neatly place about ⅓ cup of the apple mixture on half of the square. Fold the pastry diagonally over the apple mixture and seal by pressing the edges of the pastry with the tines of a fork. Transfer to a sheet pan lined with parchment paper. Brush the tops with egg wash, sprinkle with sugar, make 2 small slits in each turnover, and bake for 20 minutes, until puffed and browned. Serve warm or at room temperature.

chocolate-dipped strawberries

serves 6 to 8

I confess that chocolate isn't my favorite flavor, so I'm always looking for something that will give it complexity. Coffee and vanilla are usually my first line of defense but Grand Marnier is the winner here. This chocolate dip has lots of flavor that will stand up to the sweetness of the strawberries. For a special occasion, I like to serve this after dinner with a glass of demi-sec champagne or more Grand Marnier liqueur.

6 tablespoons heavy cream
1 teaspoon grated orange zest
7 ounces semisweet chocolate, such as Callebaut, chopped
1/2 teaspoon instant coffee granules
3 tablespoons Grand Marnier liqueur
2 tablespoons light corn syrup
Long-stemmed strawberries, for serving

In a heat-proof bowl set over (but not touching) simmering water, heat the cream and orange zest. Add the chocolate, coffee, Grand Marnier, and corn syrup and stir constantly until the chocolate is just melted and smooth. Keep the chocolate warm in a fondue pot or in a glass bowl set over the simmering water. Serve the warm chocolate with a large plate of long-stemmed strawberries for dipping.

french chocolate bark

makes 18 to 20 pieces

There are all kinds of methods for "tempering" chocolate and I don't have the patience for most of them. This method in the microwave seems to work and it's so easy. In the U.S., chocolate bark is made by mixing raisins and nuts into warm chocolate. In France, the raisins and nuts are embedded on top, which looks so much more delicious.

For the holidays, we used this recipe for very elegant s'mores around a fire pit. What a fun night that was!

I like Callebaut and Valrhona chocolates; they are available at specialty food stores.

> 1 cup whole salted, roasted cashews
> 6 to 7 ounces very good semisweet chocolate, finely chopped
> 6 to 7 ounces very good bittersweet chocolate, finely chopped
> 1/4 cup dried crystallized ginger, 1/2-inch diced
> 1/2 cup dried cherries
> 1/2 cup dried apricots, 1/2-inch diced
> 1/4 cup golden raisins

Preheat the oven to 350 degrees. Using a pencil, draw a 9 × 10-inch rectangle on a piece of parchment paper placed on a sheet pan, then turn the parchment paper over.

Spread the cashews in one layer on another sheet pan and bake for 8 minutes. Set aside to cool.

Place the semisweet chocolate and half the bittersweet chocolate in a glass bowl and microwave on high power for 20 to 30 seconds. (Don't trust your microwave timer; time it with your watch.) Stir with a rubber spatula. Continue to heat and stir in 30-second increments until the chocolate is *just* melted. Immediately add the remaining bittersweet chocolate and allow it to sit at room temperature, stirring often, until it's completely smooth. Stir vigorously until the chocolate is smooth and slightly cooled; stirring makes it glossier.

Pour the melted chocolate onto the parchment paper and spread it lightly into the drawn rectangle. Sprinkle the top evenly in the following order: first the ginger, then the cooled whole cashews, the cherries, apricots, and raisins. Set aside for 1 to 2 hours until firm. Cut the bark in 18 to 20 pieces and serve at room temperature.

old-fashioned gingerbread

serves 9

James Beard was an icon of American cooking; this gingerbread is inspired by his original recipe. It's sweet and spicy the way real gingerbread should be—with lots of molasses and chunky crystallized ginger. The orange glaze or a dollop of whipped cream flavored with rum won't hurt, either.

1/4 cup dark rum or water

1/2 cup golden raisins

1/4 pound (1 stick) unsalted butter

1 cup unsulfured molasses

1 cup (8 ounces) sour cream

1 1/2 teaspoons grated orange zest

2 1/3 cups all-purpose flour

3/4 teaspoon baking soda

1 1/2 teaspoons ground ginger

1 teaspoon ground cinnamon

1/4 teaspoon ground cloves

1/2 teaspoon kosher salt

1/3 cup minced dried crystallized ginger (not in syrup)

1 cup confectioners' sugar

2 tablespoons plus 1 teaspoon freshly squeezed orange juice

Preheat the oven to 350 degrees. Grease an 8 × 8-inch cake pan and line with parchment paper. Grease and flour the pan.

Place the rum and raisins in a small pan, cover, and heat until the rum boils. Turn off the heat and set aside. Place the butter and molasses in another small pan and bring to a boil over medium heat. Pour the mixture into the bowl of an electric mixer fitted with the paddle attachment. Cool for 5 minutes, then mix in the sour cream and orange zest.

Meanwhile, sift the flour, baking soda, ginger, cinnamon, cloves, and salt together into a small bowl. Mix with your hand until combined. With the mixer on low speed, slowly add the flour mixture to the molasses mixture and mix only until smooth.

Drain the raisins and add them and the crystallized ginger to the mixture with a spatula. Pour into the prepared pan and bake for about 35 minutes, until a toothpick comes out clean. Set aside to cool completely.

When the cake is cooled, whisk together the confectioners' sugar and orange juice and pour it over the gingerbread, allowing it to drip down the sides. Allow the glaze to set. Cut the gingerbread into 9 squares.

plum crunch

serves 8

This recipe is a variation on a recipe from my friend Sarah Leah Chase, who wrote one of my favorite cookbooks, Nantucket Open-House Cookbook. *The cassis makes the plums taste more "plum-y" without making its own statement. Prune plums are only available for a few weeks in September, but regular plums are also good in summer when they're in season.*

3 pounds Italian prune plums, pitted and quartered

1½ cups light brown sugar, lightly packed

¼ cup all-purpose flour

6 tablespoons crème de cassis liqueur

FOR THE TOPPING

1½ cups all-purpose flour

¾ cup granulated sugar

¾ cup light brown sugar, lightly packed

½ teaspoon kosher salt

1 cup oatmeal

½ cup chopped walnuts

½ pound (2 sticks) cold unsalted butter, diced

Vanilla ice cream, for serving

Cassis is a liqueur made from black currants. A splash is delicious in white wine to make a kir or in champagne for a kir royale.

Preheat the oven to 375 degrees.

For the fruit, in a large bowl, combine the plums, brown sugar, flour, and cassis. Pour the mixture into a 12 × 8-inch shallow baking dish.

For the topping, combine the flour, granulated sugar, brown sugar, salt, oatmeal, walnuts, and butter in the bowl of an electric mixer fitted with the paddle attachment. Mix on low speed until the mixture is crumbly and the butter is the size of peas. Scatter evenly over the plum mixture.

Bake the plum crunch for 40 to 45 minutes, until the plums are bubbling and the top is browned. Serve warm or at room temperature with ice cream.

honey vanilla fromage blanc

serves 6 to 8

You can peel the peaches and nectarines, if you like. Blanch ripe fruit in hot water for thirty seconds and then slide the skins off.

One of our favorite restaurants in Paris is called Au Bon Accueil, which means "a warm welcome." It's wonderful to go there because the food's so good and the people are charming; but the biggest thrill is walking out on the street after dinner and looking straight up at the Eiffel Tower sparkling above. It doesn't get any more romantic! I was served this delicious dessert one night and I couldn't wait to go home and make it myself. It's a bowl of honey vanilla fromage blanc piled with fresh fruit and berries and drizzled with fresh raspberry sauce.

32 ounces *fromage blanc* (see note)
1/4 cup heavy cream
1/2 cup good honey
4 teaspoons pure vanilla extract
1/2 teaspoon freshly grated lemon zest
   Vanilla seeds scraped from 1 vanilla bean

TO ASSEMBLE, CHOOSE FROM
   Ripe stone fruit such as peaches, nectarines, plums
   Berries such as raspberries and strawberries
   Citrus fruit such as oranges, cut in segments
   Raspberry Sauce (recipe follows)

You can order fromage blanc *from the Vermont Butter and Cheese Company (see Sources).*

Stir the *fromage blanc,* cream, honey, vanilla extract, lemon zest, and vanilla seeds together in a medium bowl. Refrigerate until ready to use.

To assemble, spoon the *fromage blanc* mixture into shallow bowls. Place the fruit artfully on top and drizzle the dessert with raspberry sauce. Serve with extra raspberry sauce on the side. I find that some people like it less sweet with just a drizzle of sauce while others prefer more sauce.

raspberry sauce makes 2 cups

1 half-pint fresh raspberries
1/2 cup sugar
1 cup seedless raspberry jam (12 ounces)
1 tablespoon framboise liqueur

Combine the raspberries, sugar, and 1/4 cup water in a small saucepan. Bring to a boil, lower the heat, and simmer for 4 minutes. Pour the cooked raspberries, jam, and framboise into the bowl of a food processor fitted with the steel blade and process until very smooth. Chill.

honey vanilla pound cake

makes one 8-inch loaf

There's a magazine that I love called Cook's Illustrated. *It's not very fancy and has no glossy photographs but it does have so much fascinating information about cooking. They recommend using "cool room temperature" butter, which makes all the difference in the texture of this pound cake.*

$^{1}/_{2}$ pound (2 sticks) unsalted butter, at cool room temperature (see note)

$1^{1}/_{4}$ cups sugar

4 extra-large eggs, at room temperature

2 tablespoons honey

2 teaspoons pure vanilla extract

1 teaspoon grated lemon zest

2 cups sifted cake flour

1 teaspoon kosher salt

$^{1}/_{2}$ teaspoon baking powder

If you allow the butter to sit at room temperature for about 1 hour, it will be at "cool room temperature."

Preheat the oven to 350 degrees. Grease the bottom of an $8^{1}/_{2} \times 4^{1}/_{2} \times 2^{1}/_{2}$-inch loaf pan. Line the bottom with parchment paper, then grease and flour the pan.

In the bowl of an electric mixer fitted with the paddle attachment, cream the butter and sugar on medium speed for 3 to 4 minutes, until light. Meanwhile, put the eggs, honey, vanilla, and lemon zest in a glass measuring cup but do not combine. With the mixer on medium-low speed, add the egg mixture, one egg at a time, scraping down the bowl and allowing each egg to become incorporated before adding the next egg.

Sift together the flour, salt, and baking powder. With the mixer on low speed, add it slowly to the batter until just combined. Finish mixing the batter with a rubber spatula and pour it into the prepared pan. Smooth the top. Bake for 50 to 60 minutes, until a toothpick inserted in the center comes out clean. Cool for 15 minutes, turn out onto a baking rack, and cool completely.

fresh raspberry gratins

serves 6

Raspberry gratins are made by placing fresh raspberries in shallow gratin dishes and covering them with a rich sabayon sauce. They're placed under the broiler very quickly so the tops brown and the sugar caramelizes. It's a delicious warm dessert on a cold night; but since it's made with fresh fruit, I also love to serve it in the summer.

8 extra-large egg yolks
²/₃ cup superfine or caster sugar
1 cup sweet Marsala wine
¼ teaspoon pure vanilla extract
6 half-pints fresh raspberries
Granulated sugar

Be sure to get sweet (not dry) Marsala wine from the liquor store.

Superfine sugar is called caster (or castor) sugar in England. It dissolves quickly and can be used cup for cup in place of granulated sugar in almost any recipe.

Preheat the broiler for at least 15 minutes, with the rack about 5 inches away from the heat.

To make the sabayon, whisk together the egg yolks and sugar in a heat-proof bowl set over a pan of simmering (not boiling) water until thick and creamy, about 4 to 5 minutes. Whisk almost constantly, scraping the egg mixture from the bottom of the bowl. Slowly whisk in the Marsala wine and continue whisking over the simmering water for about 5 more minutes, until the mixture is thick and smooth, like a soft whipped cream. It should register about 150 degrees on an instant-read thermometer. Whisk in the vanilla, remove from the heat, and set aside.

Place one snug layer of raspberries in 6 (6- to 7-inch) shallow gratin dishes. (Each of my dishes holds about one half-pint of raspberries.) Spoon enough sabayon over the raspberries to cover them. Sprinkle each one lightly with granulated sugar. Arrange the dishes on 2 sheet pans and place them—one pan at a time—under the broiler for 2 to 3 minutes, or until the tops of the gratins are lightly browned. Watch them carefully; they burn really quickly! Serve warm.

pumpkin roulade with ginger buttercream

serves 8

I'm always looking for an alternative to the expected pumpkin pie for the holidays. I've made pumpkin mousse, pumpkin banana mousse tart, and finally I decided to make a pumpkin version of a bûche de noël. It's a pumpkin spice cake filled with a mascarpone and ginger cream. You can make it in advance and keep it refrigerated before serving.

FOR THE CAKE

- ³⁄₄ cup all-purpose flour
- ¹⁄₂ teaspoon baking powder
- ¹⁄₂ teaspoon baking soda
- 1 teaspoon ground cinnamon
- 1 teaspoon ground ginger
- ¹⁄₄ teaspoon ground nutmeg
- ¹⁄₂ teaspoon kosher salt
- 3 extra-large eggs, at room temperature
- 1 cup granulated sugar
- ³⁄₄ cup canned pumpkin (not pie filling)
- ¹⁄₄ cup confectioners' sugar, plus extra for dusting

FOR THE FILLING

- 12 ounces Italian mascarpone cheese
- 1¹⁄₄ cups sifted confectioners' sugar
- 2 tablespoons heavy cream
- ¹⁄₄ cup minced dried crystallized ginger (not in syrup)
- Pinch of kosher salt

To make in advance, wrap the filled cake in plastic wrap and refrigerate for up to 3 days. Dust with confectioners' sugar just before serving.

Preheat the oven to 375 degrees. Grease a 13 × 18 × 1-inch sheet pan. Line the pan with parchment paper and grease and flour the paper.

In a small bowl, sift together the flour, baking powder, baking soda, cinnamon, ginger, nutmeg, and salt and stir to combine. Place the eggs and granulated sugar in the bowl of an electric mixer fitted with the paddle attachment and beat on medium-high speed for 3 minutes, until light yellow and thickened. With the mixer on low, add the pumpkin, then slowly add the flour mixture, mixing just until incorporated. Finish mixing the batter by hand with a rubber spatula. Pour into the prepared pan and spread evenly. Bake the cake for 10 to 12 minutes, until the top springs back when gently touched.

While the cake is baking, lay out a clean, thin cotton dish towel on a flat surface and sift the entire $1/4$ cup of confectioners' sugar evenly over it. (This will prevent the cake from sticking to the towel.) As soon as you remove the cake from the oven, loosen it around the edges and invert it squarely onto the prepared towel. Peel away the parchment paper. With a light touch, roll the warm cake and the towel together (don't press!), starting at the short end of the cake. Allow to cool *completely* on a wire rack.

Meanwhile, make the filling. In the bowl of an electric mixer fitted with the paddle attachment, beat the mascarpone, confectioners' sugar, and cream together for about a minute, until light and fluffy. Stir in the crystallized ginger and salt.

To assemble, carefully unroll the cake onto a board with the towel underneath. Spread the cake evenly with the filling. Reroll the cake in a spiral using the towel as a guide. Remove the towel and trim the ends to make a neat edge. Dust with confectioners' sugar and serve sliced.

raisin pecan oatmeal cookies

makes 30 to 35 cookies

I consider myself an oatmeal cookie aficionado and I've been searching for decades for the perfect recipe. Finally! These are crisp on the outside and chewy on the inside with lots of chunky raisins and toasted pecans.

1½ cups pecans

½ pound (2 sticks) unsalted butter, at room temperature

1 cup dark brown sugar, lightly packed

1 cup granulated sugar

2 extra-large eggs, at room temperature

2 teaspoons pure vanilla extract

1½ cups all-purpose flour

1 teaspoon baking powder

1 teaspoon ground cinnamon

1 teaspoon kosher salt

3 cups old-fashioned oatmeal

1½ cups raisins

In cooking, little details can make a big difference in flavor. When I bake with nuts, I often toast them first to bring out their flavor.

Preheat the oven to 350 degrees.

Place the pecans on a sheet pan and bake for 5 minutes, until crisp. Set aside to cool. Chop very coarsely.

In the bowl of an electric mixer fitted with the paddle attachment, beat the butter, brown sugar, and granulated sugar together on medium-high speed until light and fluffy. With the mixer on low, add the eggs, one at a time, and the vanilla.

Sift the flour, baking powder, cinnamon, and salt together into a medium bowl. With the mixer on low, slowly add the dry ingredients to the butter mixture. Add the oats, raisins, and pecans and mix just until combined.

For larger cookies, drop 3-inch mounds and bake for 20 minutes.

For chewier cookies, allow them to cool on the pan.

Using a small ice-cream scoop or a tablespoon, drop 2-inch mounds of dough onto sheet pans lined with parchment paper. Flatten slightly with a damp hand. Bake for 12 to 15 minutes, until lightly browned. Transfer the cookies to a baking rack and cool completely.

affogato sundaes

serves 4

If I don't have any time and I need an over-the-top dessert, this twist on a classic Italian confection is the easiest thing in the world. It's a blend of cold ice cream and hot espresso with a crunch of chocolate-covered espresso beans. It's so delicious and you won't even need to serve coffee with dessert. You can use regular or decaf espresso.

1 **pint hazelnut gelato**
1 **pint vanilla gelato or vanilla ice cream (see note)**
8 **tablespoons Tia Maria or Kahlúa liqueur**
8 **tablespoons freshly brewed hot espresso (see note)**
  Sweetened Whipped Cream (page 195)
  Chocolate-covered espresso beans

Place one scoop each of hazelnut and vanilla gelato in each of 4 dessert or café au lait bowls. Spoon 2 tablespoons of Tia Maria and 2 tablespoons of hot espresso over each serving. Dollop some whipped cream onto each serving and garnish with a handful of chocolate-covered espresso beans. Serve immediately.

To brew espresso in an electric coffee-maker, use $1/3$ cup ground espresso and 4 cups water.

Defrost the ice cream in a microwave for about 30 seconds before serving. Ice cream has the most flavor when it's still frozen but just beginning to melt.

brownie pudding

serves 6

Anna Pump makes this dessert at her store Loaves & Fishes. It's rich and delicious and so easy to make. The edges bake like a brownie and the insides are like molten chocolate. Your friends really will go crazy.

I use good-quality chocolate—Callebaut or Valrhona. The cocoa powder is Pernigotti.

This dessert can be made up to 3 days in advance. Wrap well, refrigerate, and bring to room temperature before serving.

½ **pound (2 sticks) unsalted butter, plus extra for buttering the dish**

4 **extra-large eggs, at room temperature**

2 **cups sugar**

¾ **cup good cocoa powder**

½ **cup all-purpose flour**

Seeds scraped from 1 vanilla bean

1 **tablespoon framboise liqueur (optional)**

Vanilla ice cream, for serving

Preheat the oven to 325 degrees. Lightly butter a 2-quart (9 × 12 × 2-inch) oval baking dish. Melt the butter and set aside to cool.

In the bowl of an electric mixer fitted with the paddle attachment, beat the eggs and sugar on medium-high speed for 5 to 10 minutes, until very thick and light yellow. Meanwhile, sift the cocoa powder and flour together and set aside.

When the egg and sugar mixture is ready, lower the speed to low and add the vanilla seeds, framboise (if using), and the cocoa powder and flour mixture. Mix only until combined. With the mixer still on low, slowly pour in the cooled butter and mix again just until combined.

Pour the brownie mixture into the prepared dish and place it in a larger baking pan. Add enough of the hottest tap water to the pan to come halfway up the side of the dish and bake for exactly 1 hour. A cake tester inserted 2 inches from the side will come out three-quarters clean. The center will appear very under-baked; this dessert is between a brownie and a pudding.

Allow to cool and serve with vanilla ice cream.

breakfast

sunrise smoothies

country french omelet

buttermilk cheddar biscuits

baked blintzes

homemade muesli

tri-berry oven pancakes

whitefish salad

easy sticky buns

homemade granola bars

blueberry streusel muffins

date nut spice bread

fruit salad with limoncello

easy strawberry jam

bake like a pro

1 Measure all the ingredients carefully.

2 Fluff the flour with your measuring cup before you measure it.

3 Level off the measuring cup with a straight knife or metal spatula.

4 Use dry measures for dry ingredients, such as flour and sugar, and liquid measures for wet ingredients, such as milk or sour cream.

5 Bring butter and eggs fully to room temperature before using them to bake a cake. I leave them out of the refrigerator overnight, but they need at least 2 hours on the counter to come to room temperature.

6 Beat the butter, sugar, and eggs on high speed, until light and fluffy. Add the flour on low speed and, from that point on, mix the batter only as much as necessary to combine the ingredients. You don't want to develop the gluten in the flour by overbeating it.

7 Test your oven with an oven thermometer each time you bake; don't trust the dial!

8 Line your baking pans with parchment paper. There's no point in baking something if you can't get it out of the pan.

9 Bake in the middle of the oven, unless otherwise specified, for the best heat circulation, and don't overcrowd the oven.

10 Don't overbake! When a cake recipe says to bake for 20 to 25 minutes, start checking the cake with a wooden skewer after 18 minutes.

sunrise smoothies

serves 2

This breakfast treat is an explosion of fruit flavor. If you want it even easier, use frozen strawberries and peaches. It's good for a special weekend breakfast but also delicious for an afternoon pick-me-up.

1 cup chopped strawberries (5 strawberries)
1 cup chopped seeded watermelon
1 cup chopped fresh peach
1 cup (½ pint) raspberry sorbet
¼ cup freshly squeezed orange juice
   Watermelon spears, for garnish

Place the strawberries, watermelon, peach, sorbet, and orange juice in a blender and purée until smooth and creamy. Add more orange juice if you'd like it a little less thick. Serve immediately in glasses with watermelon spears.

country french omelet

serves 2

Jeffrey and I have a wonderful routine when we go to Paris. We arrive late morning, drop our bags, and rush to Café Varenne for lunch. They make this fabulous country omelet with bacon, potatoes, and chopped chives. It's such a satisfying breakfast or lunch. If you want to serve four people, double the recipe and make it in two pans.

- 1 tablespoon good olive oil
- 3 slices thick-cut bacon, cut into 1-inch pieces
- 1 cup (1-inch-diced) unpeeled Yukon Gold potatoes
  Kosher salt and freshly ground black pepper
- 5 extra-large eggs
- 3 tablespoons milk
- 1 tablespoon unsalted butter
- 1 tablespoon fresh chopped chives

Preheat the oven to 350 degrees.

Heat the olive oil in a 10-inch ovenproof omelet pan over medium heat. Add the bacon and cook for 3 to 5 minutes over medium-low heat, stirring occasionally, until the bacon is browned but not crisp. Take the bacon out of the pan with a slotted spoon and set aside on a plate.

Place the potatoes in the pan and sprinkle with salt and pepper. Continue to cook over medium-low heat for 8 to 10 minutes, until very tender and browned, tossing occasionally to brown evenly. Remove with a slotted spoon to the same plate with the bacon.

Meanwhile, in a medium bowl, beat the eggs, milk, 1/2 teaspoon salt, and 1/4 teaspoon pepper together with a fork. After the potatoes are removed, pour the fat out of the pan and discard. Add the butter, lower the heat to low, and pour the eggs into the hot pan. Sprinkle the bacon, potatoes, and chives evenly over the top and place the pan in the oven for about 8 minutes, just until the eggs are set. Slide onto a plate, divide in half, and serve hot.

buttermilk cheddar biscuits

makes 8 biscuits

The goal with biscuits is for them to be light and flaky but still moist. You can assemble these and refrigerate them overnight. Then all I have to do in the morning is sprinkle them with extra Cheddar and some flaked sea salt and pop them in the oven.

There are so many kinds of Cheddar. I like very sharp aged white Cheddar from Vermont or—if you can get it—any farmhouse Cheddar imported from Neal's Yard Dairy in London.

I sprinkle the tops with Maldon flaked sea salt before baking.

All-purpose flour
1 **tablespoon baking powder**
1½ **teaspoons kosher salt**
12 **tablespoons (1½ sticks) cold unsalted butter, diced**
½ **cup cold buttermilk, shaken**
1 **cold extra-large egg**
1 **cup grated extra-sharp Cheddar (see note)**
1 **egg beaten with 1 tablespoon water or milk**

Preheat the oven to 425 degrees.

Place 2 cups flour, the baking powder, and salt in the bowl of an electric mixer fitted with the paddle attachment. With the mixer on low, add the butter and mix until the butter is the size of peas.

Combine the buttermilk and egg in a small glass measuring cup and beat lightly with a fork. With the mixer still on low, quickly add the buttermilk mixture to the flour mixture and mix only until moistened. In a small bowl, mix the Cheddar with a small handful of flour and, with the mixer still on low, add the cheese to the dough. Mix *only* until roughly combined.

Dump out onto a well-floured board and knead lightly about six times. Roll the dough out to a rectangle 5 × 10 inches. With a sharp, floured knife, cut the dough lengthwise in half and then across in quarters, making 8 rough rectangles. Transfer to a baking sheet lined with parchment paper. Brush the tops with the egg wash, sprinkle with sea salt, and bake for 20 to 25 minutes, until the tops are browned and the biscuits are cooked through. Serve hot or warm.

baked blintzes with fresh blueberry sauce

serves 8 to 10

I love blintzes on Sunday morning, but who wants to stand at the stove first making the crepes, then making the filling, and then frying the blintzes—not to mention making the sauce? This is an easy way to have creamy blintzes baked in one dish, cut into squares, and served with a delicious fresh blueberry sauce.

FOR THE BATTER

1¹/₄ cups milk

2 tablespoons sour cream

4 tablespoons (¹/₂ stick) unsalted butter, melted

1 teaspoon pure vanilla extract

4 extra-large eggs

1¹/₃ cups all-purpose flour

2 tablespoons sugar

1 tablespoon baking powder

FOR THE FILLING

3 cups (24 ounces) ricotta cheese

8 ounces mascarpone cheese

2 extra-large eggs

¹/₃ cup sugar

1 tablespoon grated lemon zest (2 lemons)

2 tablespoons freshly squeezed lemon juice

¹/₂ teaspoon pure vanilla extract

1 teaspoon kosher salt

Fresh Blueberry Sauce (recipe follows)

Preheat the oven to 350 degrees. Butter a 9 × 13-inch cake pan or baking dish.

For the batter, place all the ingredients in the bowl of a food processor fitted with the steel blade and blend until smooth. (You can also use a blender.) Pour half the batter (about 1³/₄ cups) into the prepared dish and bake for 10 minutes, until set.

Meanwhile, for the filling, whisk together the ricotta, mascarpone, eggs, and sugar in a large bowl. Add the lemon zest, lemon juice, vanilla, and salt and mix until thoroughly combined. Spread the cheese filling over the baked pancake. Carefully spoon the remaining pancake batter to cover the cheese.

Return the pan to the oven and continue baking for 35 to 40 minutes, until the top is lightly golden and the filling is almost set. Remove from the oven and allow to stand 10 to 15 minutes. Cut the blintzes in squares and serve warm with the fresh blueberry sauce.

fresh blueberry sauce makes 2 cups

3/4 cup freshly squeezed orange juice (3 oranges)

2/3 cup sugar

1 tablespoon cornstarch

4 half-pints fresh blueberries

1 teaspoon grated lemon zest

1 tablespoon freshly squeezed lemon juice

Combine the orange juice, sugar, and cornstarch in a medium saucepan and bring to a boil, stirring occasionally. When the mixture is translucent and thickened, stir in the blueberries and simmer for 4 to 5 minutes, just until a few berries have burst but most are still whole. Stir in the lemon zest and lemon juice and cool.

homemade muesli with red berries

serves 2

Muesli is a Swiss breakfast cereal made by soaking—rather than cooking— oatmeal. It usually tastes a lot like the box it came in, but because it's so good for you, I decided to come up with muesli that actually tasted good. Toasted hazelnuts, honey, and fresh berries were just the trick. Of course, you can use any kind of fresh or dried fruit that you like, but I think this is the perfect balance.

You can use Kretschmer's Honey Crunch Wheat Germ in place of the granola.

$^1/_3$ cup quick-cooking oatmeal, preferably McCann's
$1^1/_2$ tablespoons coarsely chopped toasted hazelnuts
2 tablespoons granola with raisins (see note)
Pinch of kosher salt
$^1/_3$ cup hottest tap water
1 tablespoon honey
4 large ripe strawberries, hulled and sliced
6 to 8 fresh raspberries
2 teaspoons sugar
Greek yogurt such as Fage Total, for serving

Measure the oatmeal, hazelnuts, granola, and salt together in a cereal bowl. Pour the water and honey over the mixture, stir, and set aside to soak for 12 to 15 minutes.

Meanwhile, toss the strawberries, raspberries, and sugar together in another bowl and allow to macerate while the muesli is soaking. When ready to eat, divide the muesli between 2 bowls; divide the berries between the oat mixtures and stir in. Serve at room temperature with a dollop of yogurt on top.

tri-berry oven pancakes

serves 4

Pancakes for a crowd always presents a dilemma. Do I stand and flip them while everyone else eats or do I just make scrambled eggs instead? I decided to tackle the problem and make individual pancakes you can bake all together in the oven. They take fifteen minutes and you can WOW your family first thing in the morning.

- 1 cup *each* raspberries, blueberries, and sliced strawberries
- 1 tablespoon granulated sugar
- 2 tablespoons unsalted butter, melted, plus 4 teaspoons for the dishes
- 3 extra-large eggs, at room temperature
- ½ cup milk
- ½ cup all-purpose flour
- 1 teaspoon pure vanilla extract
- 1 teaspoon grated orange zest
- ¾ teaspoon kosher salt
- Maple syrup and confectioners' sugar, for garnish

Preheat the oven to 425 degrees.

Gently combine the berries and sugar in a small bowl and set aside while you make the pancakes. Place 4 (6- to 7-inch) individual gratin dishes on two sheet pans. Place 1 teaspoon of butter in each gratin dish and set aside.

Place the eggs in the bowl of an electric mixer fitted with a whisk attachment and beat on medium speed until mixed. Add the milk and combine. Slowly add the flour, vanilla, orange zest, 2 tablespoons melted butter, and the salt and mix just until smooth. Whisk by hand if the mixture is lumpy.

Place the gratin dishes in the oven for 3 minutes, until the butter is hot and bubbly. Make sure the butter covers the bottom of each dish. Immediately divide the batter equally among the gratin dishes and bake for 12 to 14 minutes, until puffed and lightly browned. Divide the berries among the dishes, drizzle with maple syrup, dust with confectioners' sugar, and serve hot.

My gratin dishes measure 6 inches in diameter across the bottom and 7 inches across the top.

bagels with smoked salmon & whitefish salad

serves 6

Sometimes the smallest thing can make a big difference. Years ago, I found that toasted bagels taste so much better when they're sliced in thirds instead of halves. Every time I serve them to company, they comment on it. When I was growing up, my grandparents used to drive from Brooklyn every Sunday to visit us in Connecticut and they'd bring bags of fresh bagels with smoked salmon and whitefish salad. This breakfast still reminds me of them.

$1\frac{1}{2}$ **pounds smoked whitefish, skinned and boned**
$\frac{1}{2}$ **cup minced red onion**
$\frac{1}{2}$ **cup minced celery**
1 **cup good mayonnaise**
$1\frac{1}{2}$ **tablespoons freshly squeezed lemon juice**
$\frac{3}{4}$ **teaspoon kosher salt**
$\frac{1}{4}$ **teaspoon freshly ground black pepper**

FOR SERVING

6 **bagels, sliced in thirds horizontally**
1 **pound thinly sliced smoked salmon**
16 **ounces cream cheese, softened**
Sliced tomatoes and thinly sliced red onions

With your hands, flake the whitefish, being careful to discard all the skin and bones. In a medium bowl, gently combine the whitefish with the red onion, celery, mayonnaise, lemon juice, salt, and pepper. Taste for seasoning.

Toast the bagel slices in a toaster. Arrange a platter with the smoked salmon, cream cheese, tomatoes, and red onions. Serve with the whitefish salad at room temperature.

easy sticky buns

makes 12

We used to make really delicious sticky buns at Barefoot Contessa, but they took two days to make because the yeast dough needed to rise overnight in the refrigerator. I was dying to find a way to make them easier, so I decided to try baking them with Pepperidge Farm puff pastry dough instead. OMG are they good . . . and they're really easy to make! Light, flaky dough filled with brown sugar, toasted pecans, and sweet raisins—my friends go crazy when I make these.

12 tablespoons (1½ sticks) unsalted butter, at room temperature
⅓ cup light brown sugar, lightly packed
½ cup pecans, chopped in very large pieces
1 package (17.3 ounces/2 sheets) frozen puff pastry, defrosted

FOR THE FILLING

2 tablespoons unsalted butter, melted and cooled
⅔ cup light brown sugar, lightly packed
3 teaspoons ground cinnamon
1 cup raisins

Preheat the oven to 400 degrees. Place a 12-cup standard muffin tin on a sheet pan lined with parchment paper.

In the bowl of an electric mixer fitted with the paddle attachment, combine the 12 tablespoons butter and ⅓ cup brown sugar. Place 1 rounded tablespoon of the mixture in each of the 12 muffin cups. Distribute the pecans evenly among the 12 muffin cups on top of the butter and sugar mixture.

Lightly flour a wooden board or stone surface. Unfold one sheet of puff pastry with the folds going left to right. Brush the whole sheet with half of the melted butter. Leaving a 1-inch border on the puff pastry, sprinkle each sheet with ⅓ cup of the brown sugar, 1½ teaspoons of the cinnamon, and ½ cup of the raisins. Starting with the end nearest you, roll the pastry up snugly like a jelly roll around the filling, finishing the roll with the seam side down. Trim the ends of the roll about ½ inch and discard. Slice the roll in 6 equal pieces, each about $1\frac{1}{2}$ inches wide. Place each piece, spiral side up, in 6 of the muffin cups. Repeat with the second sheet of puff pastry to make 12 sticky buns.

Bake for 30 minutes, until the sticky buns are golden to dark brown on top and firm to the touch. Allow to cool for *5 minutes only*, invert the buns onto the parchment paper (ease the filling and pecans out onto the buns with a spoon), and cool completely.

homemade granola bars

makes 12 to 16 bars

I have a thing about commercial granola bars. They all claim to contain fruit and granola but if you read the fine print, you'll see that they also have ten different kinds of corn syrup. I'd much rather make my own granola bars with real oats, almonds, and dried fruit. These are even better the second day.

2 cups old-fashioned oatmeal
1 cup sliced almonds
1 cup shredded coconut, loosely packed
1/2 cup toasted wheat germ
3 tablespoons unsalted butter
2/3 cup honey
1/4 cup light brown sugar, lightly packed
1 1/2 teaspoons pure vanilla extract
1/4 teaspoon kosher salt
1/2 cup chopped pitted dates
1/2 cup chopped dried apricots
1/2 cup dried cranberries

Preheat the oven to 350 degrees. Butter an 8 × 12-inch baking dish and line it with parchment paper.

Toss the oatmeal, almonds, and coconut together on a sheet pan and bake for 10 to 12 minutes, stirring occasionally, until lightly browned. Transfer the mixture to a large mixing bowl and stir in the wheat germ.

Reduce the oven temperature to 300 degrees.

Place the butter, honey, brown sugar, vanilla, and salt in a small saucepan and bring to a boil over medium heat. Cook and stir for a minute, then pour over the toasted oatmeal mixture. Add the dates, apricots, and cranberries and stir well.

Pour the mixture into the prepared pan. Wet your fingers and lightly press the mixture evenly into the pan. Bake for 25 to 30 minutes, until light golden brown. Cool for at least 2 to 3 hours before cutting into squares. Serve at room temperature.

blueberry streusel muffins

makes 20 muffins

Blueberry muffins were always the most popular muffins at Barefoot Contessa. I wanted to add some texture to them so I made these with a streusel topping. Buttermilk makes these muffins moist and the blueberries make them sweet. The lemon zest gives them depth of flavor; you're not aware that it's there, only that they're really delicious muffins.

3½ cups all-purpose flour
1½ cups granulated sugar
4½ teaspoons baking powder
1 teaspoon baking soda
1 teaspoon kosher salt
2 cups buttermilk, shaken
¼ pound (1 stick) unsalted butter, melted and cooled
1½ teaspoons grated lemon zest
2 extra-large eggs
2 cups fresh blueberries (2 half-pints)

FOR THE STREUSEL TOPPING
¾ cup all-purpose flour
½ cup light brown sugar, lightly packed
1 teaspoon ground cinnamon
¼ teaspoon kosher salt
4 tablespoons (½ stick) cold unsalted butter, diced

Wash blueberries in a strainer under running water and pick out any stems and leaves.

Preheat the oven to 375 degrees. Line muffin tins with paper liners.

Sift the flour, sugar, baking powder, baking soda, and salt into a large bowl and blend with your hands. In a separate bowl, whisk together the buttermilk, butter, lemon zest, and eggs. Stir the buttermilk mixture into the flour mixture with a fork, mixing just until blended. Fold the blueberries into the batter. Don't overmix! With a standard (2¼-inch) ice-cream scoop or large spoon, scoop the batter into the prepared cups, filling them almost full.

For the topping, place all the ingredients in the bowl of a food processor fitted with the steel blade and pulse until the butter is in very small pieces. Pour into a bowl and rub with your fingers until crumbly. Spoon about 1 tablespoon of the streusel on top of each muffin. Bake the muffins for 20 to 25 minutes, until golden brown.

date nut spice bread

makes 1 (8-inch) loaf

Everyone's mother had a recipe for date nut bread, but I thought it would be fun to turn up the volume and make the best one you ever ate. This rich cake is filled with dates and nuts and is served with an orange cream cheese spread on the side. Be sure to zest the oranges before you juice them.

To store, wrap tightly in plastic wrap and refrigerate the bread and the cream cheese spread separately for up to a week.

2 cups coarsely chopped dates (10 ounces pitted)

$^1/_3$ cup Cointreau or Triple Sec

4 tablespoons ($^1/_2$ stick) unsalted butter, at room temperature

$^3/_4$ cup light brown sugar, lightly packed

1 extra-large egg

1 teaspoon pure vanilla extract

1 tablespoon grated orange zest (2 oranges)

2 cups all-purpose flour

2 teaspoons baking powder

$^1/_2$ teaspoon baking soda

1 teaspoon ground cinnamon

1 teaspoon ground nutmeg

$^1/_4$ teaspoon ground cloves

1 teaspoon kosher salt

$^3/_4$ cup freshly squeezed orange juice (3 oranges)

$^3/_4$ cup coarsely chopped pecans (3 ounces)

FOR THE CREAM CHEESE SPREAD

6 ounces cream cheese, at room temperature

$^1/_3$ cup granulated sugar

1 tablespoon grated orange zest

Preheat the oven to 350 degrees. Butter the bottom of an $8^1/_2 \times 4^1/_2 \times 2^1/_2$-inch loaf pan. Line the bottom with parchment paper, then butter and flour the pan.

Combine the dates and Cointreau in a small bowl and set aside for 30 minutes. Stir occasionally.

In the bowl of an electric mixer fitted with the paddle attachment, beat the butter and brown sugar together on medium speed for 1 minute. Scrape down the bowl. With the mixer on low, add the egg, vanilla, and orange zest. Sift together the flour, baking powder, baking soda, cinnamon, nutmeg, cloves, and salt. With the mixer still on low, add the flour mixture alternately with the orange juice to the creamed mixture, beating only until combined. By hand, stir in the dates with their liquid, and the pecans.

Pour the batter into the prepared loaf pan and smooth the top. Bake for 50 to 60 minutes, until a toothpick comes out clean. Cool in the pan for 10 minutes, then turn out onto a wire rack and cool completely.

Meanwhile, in the bowl of an electric mixer fitted with the paddle attachment, cream the cream cheese, sugar, and orange zest on medium speed until just combined.

Slice the bread and serve with the orange cream cheese on the side for spreading.

fruit salad with limoncello

serves 6

I'm always looking for that subtle flavor that wakes up all the other flavors in a dish. I particularly like when you're not aware of the trick; it just tastes better than you expect. That's what a splash of limoncello did for these fresh berries. A topping of thick Greek yogurt mixed with lemon curd and honey made it a breakfast good enough for company.

Limoncello is an Italian liqueur that is infused with lemon rinds.

Greek yogurt is thickened yogurt. If you can't find it, place 12 ounces of plain yogurt in a sieve lined with cheesecloth and drain over a bowl until it's thickened to the consistency of crème fraîche or sour cream. Discard the liquid.

7 ounces Greek yogurt, such as Fage Total
$^1/_3$ cup good bottled lemon curd
1 tablespoon honey
$^1/_4$ teaspoon pure vanilla extract
2 cups sliced strawberries (1 pint)
1 cup raspberries ($^1/_2$ pint)
1 cup blueberries ($^1/_2$ pint)
2 tablespoons sugar
3 tablespoons limoncello liqueur
1 banana, sliced
Fresh mint sprigs

For the lemon yogurt topping, whisk together the yogurt, lemon curd, honey, and vanilla and set aside at room temperature.

For the fruit salad, carefully toss together the strawberries, raspberries, blueberries, sugar, and limoncello. Allow them to stand at room temperature for about 5 minutes to let the berries macerate with the sugar and liqueur. Gently fold the banana into the mixture.

Serve bowls of fruit with a dollop of lemon yogurt on top. Top with a sprig of fresh mint.

easy strawberry jam

makes 3 cups

I always think of jam as something that has to cook for hours and must be watched carefully so it doesn't burn. This strawberry jam is so easy to make and it's delicious even in winter, when the strawberries aren't particularly flavorful. Pectin is what makes jams gel and it's found in underripe fruit. Granny Smith apples are available year-round and have lots of natural pectin. A handful of blueberries adds depth of flavor and color.

3 pints fresh strawberries
3 cups superfine sugar (see note)
2 tablespoons Grand Marnier or other orange-flavored liqueur
$\frac{1}{2}$ Granny Smith apple, peeled, cored, and small-diced
$\frac{1}{2}$ cup fresh blueberries

If you can't find superfine sugar, you can use caster sugar or pour granulated sugar into a food processor fitted with the steel blade and process until finely ground.

Place the strawberries in a colander and rinse them under cold running water. Drain and hull the strawberries. Cut the larger berries in half or quarters and leave the small berries whole. Place the strawberries in a deep, heavy-bottomed pot such as Le Creuset and toss them with the sugar and Grand Marnier.

Bring the berry mixture to a boil over medium heat, stirring often. Add the apple and blueberries and continue to keep the mixture at a rolling boil, stirring occasionally, until the jam reaches 220 degrees on a candy thermometer. This should take 25 to 35 minutes. Skim and discard any foam that rises to the top. Allow the mixture to cool to room temperature and then store covered in the refrigerator. It will keep refrigerated for at least 2 weeks. To keep the jam longer, pack and seal in canning jars according to the manufacturer's instructions.

top 10 flavor boosters

1 Salting meats and poultry as soon as you bring them home from the store, before rewrapping and storing.

2 Roasting, either at very high temperature for caramelizing, or at low temperature for concentrating flavor.

3 Marinating foods to be grilled in olive oil, lemon juice, soy sauce, mustard, or fresh herbs.

4 Searing meats and poultry to caramelize the surface and seal in the juices.

5 Allowing meats and poultry to "rest" before carving, so the juices settle back into the meat.

6 Cooking with seasonal ingredients whenever possible.

7 Aged Reggiano Parmesan cheese, either ground, grated, or shaved.

8 Adding freshly grated lemon zest and orange zest whenever the juice is used.

9 Adding coffee or espresso to deepen the flavor of chocolate.

10 A final sprinkle of Maldon sea salt or French fleur de sel just before a dish is served.

FAQs

Over the years I've been asked so many basic questions about cooking that I thought I'd compile a Frequently Asked Questions list. I imagine that if one person has the question, many more are also wondering about it. This is just a sample. For a constantly evolving list, please visit BarefootContessa.com.

Q. When a recipe calls for room-temperature butter and eggs, how long should you—and can you—leave them out of the refrigerator?

A. *Baking is so much better with room-temperature ingredients. The butter and eggs whip much lighter—which means a lighter cake—and the dry ingredients incorporate much more readily. I leave butter and eggs out over-night but at least 2 hours is necessary. Don't worry about them spoiling; eggs are hermetically sealed by a shell that doesn't allow bacteria to get in, and butter is all fat, which doesn't support bacteria.*

Q. Why do you use extra-large eggs?

A. *This comes from my experience running a specialty food store. Extra-large eggs have slightly more egg per dollar than any other size (which makes a big difference when you are going through 200 dozen a week). However, my assistant, Barbara, said that her baking got better when she started using extra-large eggs. It's certainly worth a try.*

Q. How do I measure a baking pan—from the inside or the outside?

A. *It makes me crazy. Each manufacturer measures a baking pan differently. I always measure from the outside dimension—outside the top lip of the pan, not including any handles. A standard sheet pan (which is professionally called a half-sheet pan) is about 12 × 18 inches, but it's actually 13⅛ × 18⅜).*

Q. What's kosher?

A. *I know I'm going to get myself in trouble for this answer because kosher means different things to different people. Some people observe the Jewish tradition of not eating pork or shellfish, which means no bacon, sausage, lobster, or shrimp, to name a few things. A more strict interpretation is based on the belief that you should never cook a calf in its mother's milk, so people who adhere to this tradition never eat meat and dairy products in the same meal. For example, if they have chicken for dinner, it would never be served in a cream sauce, and if they have a steak, they wouldn't have ice cream for dessert. People who keep a very strict kosher kitchen have two sets of dishes—one for meat meals and one for dairy meals.*

Q. What is kosher salt?

A. *The term koshering refers to a process of salting meat to draw out the blood. Koshering (or simply "kosher") salt is the salt that's used. It's the salt I use in almost all my cooking because it has a softer and less harsh flavor than traditional "table" salt.*

Q. If I don't have an electric stand mixer (such as a KitchenAid), can I use a hand mixer?

A. *I can't think of anything that you can't make with a hand mixer instead of a stand mixer; it just means that you have to hold the mixer instead of using that time preparing the rest of the ingredients. But yes, you can always use a hand mixer and the results will be the same.*

Q. I'm afraid to use raw eggs in a recipe. What can I substitute?

A. *So many people are worried about salmonella these days and there are a few things that you can do to reduce the risk in raw eggs. First, get your eggs at an organic or local farm where there's less likelihood of contamination. Second, for vinaigrettes, generally you can eliminate the egg or substitute a tablespoon of mustard to emulsify the dressing. Third, you can sometimes find pasteurized eggs in the grocery store that won't have any problems. For other dishes that require a raw egg, I would tend to make something else rather than worry about getting sick.*

Q. How do you defrost something like meat or a cake?

A. *The best way to defrost anything is to do it overnight in the refrigerator. This way, it defrosts slowly, which apparently does the least damage to the product, but also avoids the danger of having the outside warm and exposed to contamination while the inside is still frozen. The ideal is to keep food that can spoil under 45 degrees and defrosting it in the refrigerator will keep it there.*

Q. How do I reheat a baguette?

A. *Amazingly, the best way to reheat a baguette is to run it quickly under the tap with the water running and then put it directly into a 350-degree oven for about 10 minutes, until it's crisp on the outside and warm on the inside.*

Q. What do you mean by "good" mayonnaise and "good" olive oil?

A. *I'm clearly big on using good ingredients, but that doesn't necessarily mean they have to be expensive ingredients. For mayonnaise, I use Hellmann's or Duke's. For olive oil, I use Olio Santo olive oil from California. The way I choose ingredients is this: If I'm wondering which bottle I'd prefer, I'll buy all of them at one time. I take them home, taste all of them together, and then I know forever which mayonnaise or olive oil I like best. Nothing's wasted— I'll use all the bottles at some point—but I'll never wonder again which mayonnaise to choose.*

Q. I have a convection oven; how do I convert recipes for a conventional oven to make them in my oven?

A. *At Barefoot Contessa, we only used convection ovens and they're great for almost anything except baking very light cakes, which tend to be pulled toward the fan. For most recipes, I'd start by reducing the temperature by 25 degrees and reducing the cooking time by 10 percent.*

Q. Whenever I buy fresh herbs it seems like I use a tablespoon and then waste the rest of the bunch. Should I use dried herbs, instead?

A. *I personally prefer fresh herbs; they have so much more flavor. I chop the amount of herbs that I need for a recipe and then chop the rest of the bunch and freeze it in small containers to use at another time. That way you get all of the flavor and none of the waste. This works well for thyme, rosemary, dill, parsley, and most green herbs. It's not so good for basil, which will turn brown in the freezer. The best way to preserve basil is to make pesto, cover it with a film of oil, and freeze it in small containers.*

Q. I'm not a great baker. What can I do to change that?

A. *I think the root of many baking disasters is how you measure ingredients. For cooking, the measuring isn't so critical, but for baking, it's very important to be exact. Always use a liquid measuring cup for wet ingredients—milk, maple syrup, molasses, oil—and dry measures for dry ingredients—flour, sugar, cornstarch, and nuts. For flour, rather than sifting flour before I measure it, I fluff the flour with my metal measuring cup and then carefully scoop more than enough flour into the cup. Without tapping the cup at all, I use a straight metal edge such as the back of a knife to level off the cup.*

Q. I don't use any alcohol at all. What can I substitute in a recipe that calls for something like Cognac?

A. *I like the edge and flavor that alcohol brings to some dishes, such as beef bourguignon or coq au vin. However, as long as the alcohol isn't a predominant ingredient, such as peaches in Sauternes, just eliminate the alcohol and adjust the seasonings as you cook. It will still be delicious.*

Q. Some of your recipes call for superfine sugar, but I'm having a hard time finding it in my grocery store.

A. *Superfine sugar is traditionally used for making cocktails but if you can't find it, there are two options. First, you can take granulated sugar and grind it finer in the bowl of a food processor fitted with the steel blade. Otherwise, it may be in your grocery or specialty food store under the name "caster sugar" or "castor sugar," which is the British term for superfine sugar.*

Q. I love to make your filet of beef (from *Barefoot Contessa Parties*) but my oven smokes when I cook it. What should I do?

A. *Unfortunately, the best temperature to cook a filet of beef is at 500 degrees, which is a really hot oven. It's not the filet that's smoking, it's any residue left in the oven. So, the only thing I can recommend is to be sure your oven is very clean before you make the filet. Believe me, it's worth the extra effort!*

credits

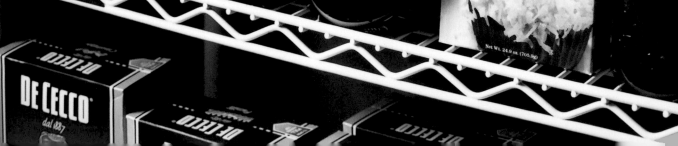

sources

SPECIALTY FOODS

Specialty food stores:

Eli's Manhattan
1411 Third Avenue
New York, New York 10028
(212) 717-8100
EliZabar.com

Dean & Deluca
560 Broadway
New York, New York 10012
Other locations: Saint Helena,
California; Kansas City, Kansas;
Washington, D.C.; Charlotte,
North Carolina
(212) 226-6800
DeanandDeluca.com

My favorite breads by mail:

Eli's Breads
EliZabar.com

Poilâne Bakery
8, rue du Cherche-Midi
Paris, France
Poilane.fr

Specialty produce by mail:

Melissa's
(800) 588-0151
Melissas.com

Apples, pears, and peaches in season:

The Milk Pail
1346 Montauk Highway
Water Mill, New York 11976
(631) 726-4565
Milk-pail.com

Cheeses, mascarpone, and fromage blanc:

Cavaniola's Cheese Shop
89B Division Street
Sag Harbor, New York 11963
(631) 725-0095
Aged Pecorino and Neal's Yard
Dairy cheeses

Zingerman's
422 Detroit Street
Ann Arbor, Michigan 48108
(888) 636-8162
Zingermans.com

Neal's Yard Dairy
17 Short Gardens
Covent Garden
London, England WC2H 9UP
NealsYardDairy.co.uk

Cabot Cheddar
CabotCheese.com

Vermont Butter & Cheese Company
(800) 884-6287
ButterAndCheese.net

Mecox Bay Dairy
855 Mecox Road
Bridgehampton, New York 11932
(631) 537-0338
Homemade cheeses and
homegrown turkeys

Truffle butters, specialty meats, and poultry:

D'Artagnan
(800) 327-8246 x 0
dartagnan.com

COOKWARE & TABLEWARE

Bridge Kitchenware
711 Third Avenue
New York, New York 10017
(212) 688-4220
BridgeKitchenware.com

Crate & Barrel
Stores nationwide
CrateAndBarrel.com

Sur La Table
Stores nationwide
SurLaTable.com

Williams-Sonoma
Stores nationwide
Williams-Sonoma.com

Cassandra's Kitchen
CassandrasKitchen.com

TABLE LINENS

Bergdorf Goodman, 7th floor
754 Fifth Avenue
New York, New York 10019
(212) 753-7300
BergdorfGoodman.com

ABH Design
954A Lexington Avenue
New York, New York 10021
(212) 249-2276

Loaves & Fishes Cookshop
2422 Montauk Highway
Bridgehampton, New York 11932
(631) 537-6066
LAndFCookshop.com

For other sources, including Barefoot Contessa baking mixes and marinades, please contact us at
BarefootContessa.com.

barn sources and resources

So many people have e-mailed me to ask about details in the new barn that I thought I'd list all the wonderful people who designed it, built it, and generally worked on it with me. Thank you, everyone, for making it such a joyous project.

Architect	Frank Greenwald 62 McGuirk Street East Hampton, New York 11937 (631) 329-1567	Appliances	Viking Range 111 Front Street Greenwood, Mississippi 38930 (662) 455-1200 VikingRange.com
Interior design	Robert Stilin Red Horse Plaza 74 Montauk Highway East Hampton, New York 11937 (631) 329-7141	Hardware	Nanz Hardware 213 East 59th Street New York, New York 10022 (212) 755-5484 Nanz.com
Garden design	Joseph W. Tyree 1668 Sag Harbor Turnpike Sag Harbor, New York 11963 (631) 725-8875 JosephWTyree.com	Paint	Farrow & Ball Farrow-Ball.com Color: light gray
		Fire bowl	Elena Colombo Firefeatures (718) 399-2233 Firefeatures.com
Outdoor lighting	Greg Yale Associates Illumination 27 Henry Road Southampton, New York 11968 (631) 287-2132 GregYale.com	Outdoor sconces	Ann Morris Antiques 329 East 60th Street New York, New York 10020 (212) 755-3308 to the trade only
Indoor lighting	Tom Richmond 79 Long View Avenue White Plains, New York 10605 (914) 428-2511		
		Glass votives	Bloom 43 Madison Street Sag Harbor, New York 11963 (631) 725-5940
Construction	Ken Wright Wright & Company 17 Foster Avenue Bridgehampton, New York 11932 (631) 537-2555	Antique chairs	Bloom (above), and Amy Perlin Antiques 306 East 61st Street New York, New York 10065 (212) 593-5756 AmyPerlinAntiques.com
Landscape contractor	Michael Derrig Landscape Details 1796 Sag Harbor Turnpike Sag Harbor, New York 11968 (631) 725-0018	Cupboard	Axel Vervoordt Antiques Antwerp, Belgium Axel-Vervoordt.com

menus

breakfast

Country French Omelet (page 227)
Toasted baguettes
Fruit Salad with Limoncello (page 248)
Coffee

Freshly squeezed orange juice
Scrambled eggs
Toast with Easy Strawberry Jam (page 250)
Date Nut Spice Bread (page 246)

Sunrise Smoothies (page 224)
Baked Blintzes with Fresh Blueberry Sauce (page 230)
Fresh fruit platter
Coffee

lunch

Chilled Cucumber Soup with Shrimp (page 66)
Tomato & Goat Cheese Tarts (page 92)
Green salad with vinaigrette
Raisin Pecan Oatmeal Cookies (page 214)
Vanilla ice cream

Truffled Filet of Beef Sandwiches (page 94)
Roasted Tomato Caprese Salad (page 90)
Honey Vanilla Fromage Blanc (page 206)

Kir royale
Roasted Potato Leek Soup (page 63)
Mâche with Warm Brie & Apples (page 98)
French Apple Tart (page 191)

Campari Orange Spritzers (page 33)
Pappa al Pomodoro (page 68)
White Pizzas with Arugula (page 82)
Affogato Sundaes (page 217)

dinner

Tuscan Lemon Chicken (page 106)
Roasted Tomatoes with Basil (page 183)
Confetti Corn (page 160)
Brownie Pudding (page 218)

Roasted Turkey Roulade (page 109)
Celery Root & Apple Purée (page 169)
Maple-Roasted Butternut Squash (page 158)
Pumpkin Roulade with Ginger Buttercream (page 212)

Baked Shrimp Scampi (page 128)
Roasted Tomato Caprese Salad (page 90)
French baguettes
Plum Crunch (page 205)

Roasted capon
Tagliarelle with Truffle Butter (page 152)
Roasted carrots
French Apple Tart (page 191)

Niman Ranch Burgers (page 120)
Creamy Cucumber Salad (page 85)
Baked Sweet Potato "Fries" (page 180)
Fresh Lemon Mousse (page 194)

French Bistro Steaks with Provençal Butter
    (page 122)
Baked Potatoes with Yogurt & Sour Cream (page 166)
Roasted Parsnips & Carrots (page 179)
Apple Dried Cherry Turnovers (page 196)

For menus using recipes
from all the Barefoot
Contessa books, please go to
BarefootContessa.com.

index

recipe index